The Last Yankee

With a new essay
About Theatre Language

and

Broken Glass

BY ARTHUR MILLER

DRAMA
The Golden Years
The Man Who Had All the Luck
All My Sons
Death of a Salesman
An Enemy of the People *(adaptation of the play by Ibsen)*
The Crucible
A View from the Bridge
After the Fall
Incident at Vichy
The Price
The American Clock
The Creation of the World and Other Business
The Archbishop's Ceiling
The Ride Down Mt. Morgan

ONE-ACT PLAYS
A View from the Bridge; *one-act version, with* A Memory of Two Mondays
Elegy for a Lady *(in* Two-Way Mirror)
Some Kind of Love Story *(in* Two-Way Mirror)
I Can't Remember Anything *(in* Danger: Memory!)
Clara *(in* Danger: Memory!)
The Last Yankee

OTHER WORKS
Situation Normal
The Misfits *(a cinema novel)*
Focus *(a novel)*
I Don't Need You Anymore *(short stories)*
Theatre Essays
Chinese Encounters *(reportage with Inge Morath photographs)*
In the Country *(reportage with Inge Morath photographs)*
In Russia *(reportage with Inge Morath photographs)*
Salesman in Beijing *(a memoir)*
Timebends *(autobiography)*

COLLECTIONS
Arthur Miller's Collected Plays (Volumes I and II)
The Portable Arthur Miller
The Theater Essays of Arthur Miller *(Robert Martin, editor)*

VIKING CRITICAL LIBRARY EDITIONS
Death of a Salesman *(edited by Gerald Weales)*
The Crucible *(edited by Gerald Weales)*

TELEVISION
Playing for Time

SCREENPLAYS
The Misfits
Everybody Wins
The Crucible

The Last Yankee

With a new essay
About Theatre Language

and

Broken Glass

ARTHUR MILLER

The Fireside Theatre
Garden City, New York

THE LAST YANKEE and BROKEN GLASS
were originally published separately by
PENGUIN BOOKS

Penguin Books USA Inc., 375 Hudson Street,
New York, New York 10014, U.S.A.
Penguin Books Ltd, 27 Wrights Lane, London W8 5TZ, England
Penguin Books Australia Ltd, Ringwood, Victoria, Australia
Penguin Books Canada Ltd, 10 Alcorn Avenue,
Toronto, Ontario, Canada M4V 3B2
Penguin Books (N.Z.) Ltd, 182–190 Wairau Road,
Auckland 10, New Zealand

Penguin Books Ltd, Registered Offices;
Harmondsworth, Middlesex, England

First published in Great Britain by Methuen Drama,
an imprint of Reed Consumer Books Ltd. 1993
This edition with a new essay by Arthur Miller
published in Penguin Books 1994

CAUTION

ISBN: 1-56865-104-X

To Inge Morath

To Baby Noemh.

CONTENTS

The Last Yankee

    A Note on the Play   3

    Cast of Characters   5

About Theatre Language   58

Broken Glass   77

    Cast of Characters   79

The Last Yankee

With a new essay
About Theatre Language

A NOTE ON THE PLAY

The Last Yankee received its premiere at the Manhattan Theatre Club, New York, on January 21, 1993, with the following cast:

Leroy Hamilton	John Heard
John Frick	Tom Aldredge
Patricia Hamilton	Frances Conroy
Karen Frick	Rose Gregorio
Unnamed Patient	Charlotte Maier

Directed by John Tillinger
Set design by John Lee Beatty
Costume design by Jane Greenwood
Lighting design by Dennis Parichy
Sound design by Scott Lehrer

The play received its British premiere at the Young Vic Theatre, London, on January 26, 1993, with the following cast:

Leroy Hamilton	Peter Davison
John Frick	David Healy
Patricia Hamilton	Zoë Wanamaker
Karen Frick	Helen Burns

Directed by David Thacker
Set design by Sheilagh Keegan
Costume design by Helen Skillicorn
Lighting design by Jim Simmons
Movement by Lesley Hutchinson

CAST OF CHARACTERS

Leroy Hamilton

John Frick

Patricia Hamilton

Karen Frick

Unnamed patient

SCENE ONE

---

*The visiting room of a state mental hospital. Leroy Hamilton is
seated on one of the half-dozen chairs, idly leafing through an old
magazine. He is forty-eight, trim, dressed in subdued Ivy League
jacket and slacks and shined brogans. A banjo case rests against his
chair.*

*Mr. Frick enters. He is sixty, solid, in a business suit. He carries a
small valise. He looks about, glances at Leroy, just barely nods, and
sits ten feet away. He looks at his watch, then impatiently at the
room. Leroy goes on leafing through the magazine.*

FRICK, *pointing right:* Supposed to notify somebody in there?

LEROY, *indicating left:* Did you give your name to the attendant?

FRICK: Yes. 'Seem to be paying much attention, though.

LEROY: They know you're here, then. He calls through to the ward.
Returns to his magazine.

FRICK, *slight pause:* Tremendous parking space down there. 'They
need that for?

LEROY: Well a lot of people visit on weekends. Fills up pretty much.

FRICK: Really? That whole area?

LEROY: Pretty much.

FRICK: 'Doubt that. *He goes to the window and looks out. Pause.* Beautifully landscaped, got to say that for it.

LEROY: Yes, it's a very nice place.

FRICK: 'See them walking around out there it's hard to tell. 'Stopped one to ask directions and only realized when he stuck out his finger and pointed at my nose.

LEROY: Heh-heh.

FRICK: Quite a shock. Sitting there reading some thick book and crazy as a coot. You'd never know. *He sits in another chair. Leroy returns to the magazine. He studies Leroy.* Is it your wife?

LEROY: Yes.

FRICK: I've got mine in there too.

LEROY: Uh, huh. *He stares ahead, politely refraining from the magazine.*

FRICK: My name's Frick.

LEROY: Hi. I'm Hamilton.

FRICK: Gladameetu. *Slight pause.* How do you find it here?

LEROY: I guess they do a good job.

FRICK: Surprisingly well kept for a state institution.

LEROY: Oh, ya.

FRICK: Awful lot of colored, though, ain't there?

LEROY: Quite a few, ya.

FRICK: Yours been in long?

LEROY: Going on seven weeks now.

FRICK: They give you any idea when she can get out?

LEROY: Oh, I could take her out now, but I won't for a couple weeks.

FRICK: Why's that?

LEROY: Well this is her third time.

FRICK: 'Don't say.

LEROY: I'd like them to be a little more sure before I take her out again. . . . Although you can never *be* sure.

FRICK: That fairly common? —that they have to come back?

LEROY: About a third they say. This your first time, I guess.

FRICK: I just brought her in last Tuesday. I certainly hope she doesn't have to stay long. They ever say what's wrong with her?

LEROY: She's a depressive.

FRICK: Really. That's what they say about mine. Just gets . . . sort of sad?

LEROY: It's more like . . . frightened.

FRICK: Sounds just like mine. Got so she wouldn't even leave the house.

LEROY: That's right.

FRICK: Oh, yours too?

LEROY: Ya, she wouldn't go out. Not if she could help it, anyway.

FRICK: She ever hear sounds?

LEROY: She used to. Like a loud humming.

FRICK: Same thing! Ts. What do you know! —How old is she?

LEROY: She's forty-four.

FRICK: Is that all! I had an idea it had something to do with getting old . . .

LEROY: I don't think so. My wife is still—I wouldn't say a raving beauty, but she's still . . . a pretty winsome woman. They're usually sick a long time before you realize it, you know. I just never realized it.

FRICK: Mine never showed any signs at all. Just a nice, quiet kind of a woman. Always slept well . . .

LEROY: Well mine sleeps well too.

FRICK: Really?

LEROY: Lot of them love to sleep. I found that out. She'd take naps every afternoon. Longer and longer.

FRICK: Mine too. But then about six, eight months ago she got nervous about keeping the doors locked. And then the windows. I had to air-condition the whole house. I finally had to do the shopping, she just wouldn't go out.

LEROY: Oh I've done the shopping for twenty years.

FRICK: You don't say!

LEROY: Well you just never think of it as a sickness. I like to ski, for instance, or ice skating . . . she'd never come along. Or swimming in the summer. I always took the kids alone . . .

FRICK: Oh you have children.

LEROY: Yes. Seven.

FRICK: Seven!—I've been wondering if it was because she never had any.

LEROY: No, that's not it. —You don't have *any?*

FRICK: No. We kept putting it off, and then it got too late, and first thing you know . . . it's just too late.

LEROY: For a while there I thought maybe she had too *many* children . . .

FRICK: Well I don't have any, so . . .

LEROY: Yeah, I guess that's not it either.

Slight pause.

FRICK: I just can't figure it out. There's no bills; we're very well fixed; she's got a beautiful home. . . . There's really not a trouble in the world. Although, God knows, maybe that's the trouble . . .

LEROY: Oh no, I got plenty of bills and it didn't help mine. I don't think it's how many bills you have.

FRICK: What do you think it is, then?

LEROY: Don't ask me, I don't know.

FRICK: When she started locking up everything I thought maybe it's these Negroes, you know? There's an awful lot of fear around; all this crime.

LEROY: I don't think so. My wife was afraid before there were any Negroes. I mean, around.

FRICK: Well one thing came out of it —I finally learned how to make coffee. And mine's better than hers was. It's an awful sensation, though—coming home and there's nobody there.

LEROY: How'd you like to come home and there's seven of them there?

FRICK: I guess I'm lucky at that.

LEROY: Well, I am too. They're wonderful kids.

FRICK: They still very young?

LEROY: Five to nineteen. But they all pitch in. Everything's clean, house runs like a ship.

FRICK: You're lucky to have good children these days. —I guess we're both lucky.

LEROY: That's the only way to look at it. Start feeling sorry for yourself, that's when you're in trouble.

FRICK: Awfully hard to avoid sometimes.

LEROY: You can't give in to it though. Like tonight—I was so disgusted I just laid down and . . . I was ready to throw in the chips. But then I got up and washed my face, put on the clothes, and here I am. After all, she can't help it either, who you going to blame?

FRICK: It's a mystery—a woman with everything she could possibly want. I don't care what happens to the country, there's nothing could ever hurt her anymore. Suddenly, out of nowhere, she's terrified! . . . She lost all her optimism. Yours do that? Lose her optimism?

LEROY: Mine was never very optimistic. She's Swedish.

FRICK: Oh. Mine certainly was. Whatever deal I was in, couldn't wait till I got home to talk about it. Real estate, stock market, always interested. All of a sudden, no interest whatsoever. Might as well be talking to that wall over there. —Your wife have brothers and sisters?

LEROY: Quite a few, ya.

FRICK: Really. I even thought maybe it's that she was an only child, and if she had brothers and sisters to talk to . . .

LEROY: Oh no—at least I don't think so. It could be even worse.

FRICK: They don't help, huh?

LEROY: They *think* they're helping. Come around saying it's a disgrace for their sister to be in a public institution. That's the kind of help. So I said, "Well, I'm the public!"

FRICK: Sure! —It's a perfectly nice place.

LEROY: They want her in the Rogers Pavilion.

FRICK: Rogers! —that's a couple of hundred dollars a day minimum . . .

LEROY: Well if I had that kind of money I wouldn't mind, but . . .

FRICK: No-no, don't you do it. I could afford it, but what are we paying taxes for?

LEROY: So they can go around saying their sister's in the Rogers Pavilion, that's all.

FRICK: Out of the question. That's fifty thousand dollars a year. Plus tips. I'm sure you have to tip them there.

LEROY: Besides, it's eighty miles there and back, I could never get to see her . . .

FRICK: If they're so sensitive you ought to tell *them* to pay for it. That'd shut them up, I bet.

LEROY: Well no—they've offered to pay part. Most of it, in fact.

FRICK: Whyn't you do it, then?

LEROY, *holding a secret:* I didn't think it's a good place for her.

FRICK: Why?—if they'd pay for it? It's one of the top places in the country. Some very rich people go there.

LEROY: I know.

FRICK: And the top doctors, you know. And they order whatever they want to eat. I went up there to look it over; no question about it, it's absolutely first-class, much better than this place. You should take them up on it.

LEROY: I'd rather have her here.

FRICK: Well I admire your attitude. You don't see that kind of pride anymore.

LEROY: It's not pride, exactly.

FRICK: Never mind, it's a great thing, keep it up. Everybody's got the gimmes, it's destroying the country. Had a man in a few weeks ago to put in a new showerhead. Nothing to it. Screw off the old one and screw on the new one. Seventeen dollars an hour!

LEROY: Yeah, well. *Gets up, unable to remain seated.* Everybody's got to live, I guess.

FRICK: I take my hat off to you—that kind of independence. Don't happen to be with Colonial Trust, do you?

LEROY: No.

FRICK: There was something familiar about you. What line are you in?

LEROY, *he is at the window now, staring out. Slight pause:* Carpenter.

FRICK, *taken aback:* Don't say. . . . Contractor?

LEROY: No. Just carpenter. —I take on one or two fellas when I have to, but I work alone most of the time.

FRICK: I'd never have guessed it.

LEROY: Well that's what I do. *Looks at his watch, wanting escape.*

FRICK: I mean your whole . . . your way of dressing and everything.

LEROY: Why? Just ordinary clothes.

FRICK: No, you look like a college man.

LEROY: Most of them have long hair, don't they?

FRICK: The way college men used to look. I've spent thirty years around carpenters, that's why it surprised me. You know Frick Supply, don't you?

LEROY: Oh ya. I've bought quite a lot of wood from Frick.

FRICK: I sold out about five years ago . . .

LEROY: I know. I used to see you around there.

FRICK: You did? Why didn't you mention it?

LEROY, *shrugs:* Just didn't.

FRICK: You say Anthony?

LEROY: No, Hamilton. Leroy.

FRICK, *points at him:* Hey now! Of course! There was a big article about you in the *Herald* a couple of years ago. Descended from Alexander Hamilton.

LEROY: That's right.

FRICK: Sure! No wonder! *Holding out his palm as to a photo.* Now that I visualize you in overalls, I think I recognize you. In fact, you were out in the yard loading plywood the morning that article came out. My bookkeeper pointed you out through the window. It's those clothes—if I'd seen you in overalls I'd've recognized you right off. Well, what do you know? *The air of condescension plus wonder.* Amazing thing what clothes'll do, isn't it. —Keeping busy?

LEROY: I get work.

FRICK: What are you fellas charging now?

LEROY: I get seventeen an hour.

FRICK: Good for you.

LEROY: I hate asking that much, but even so I just about make it.

FRICK: Shouldn't feel that way; if they'll pay it, grab it.

LEROY: Well ya, but it's still a lot of money. —My head's still back there thirty years ago.

FRICK: What are you working on now?

LEROY: I'm renovating a colonial near Waverly. I just finished over in Belleville. The Presbyterian church.

FRICK: Did you do *that?*

LEROY: Yeah, just finished Wednesday.

FRICK: That's a beautiful job. You're a good man. Where'd they get that altar?

LEROY: I built that.

FRICK: That altar?

LEROY: Uh huh.

FRICK: Hell, that's first-class! Huh! You must be doing all right.

LEROY: Just keeping ahead of it.

FRICK, *slight pause:* How'd it happen?

LEROY: What's that?

FRICK: Well coming out of an old family like that—how do you come to being a carpenter?

LEROY: Just . . . liked it.

FRICK: Father a carpenter?

LEROY: No.

FRICK: What was your father?

LEROY: Lawyer.

FRICK: Why didn't you?

LEROY: Just too dumb, I guess.

FRICK: Couldn't buckle down to the books, huh?

LEROY: I guess not.

FRICK: Your father should've taken you in hand.

LEROY, *sits with magazine, opening it:* He didn't like the law either.

FRICK: Even so. —Many of the family still around?

LEROY: Well my mother, and two brothers.

FRICK: No, I mean of the Hamiltons.

LEROY: Well they're Hamiltons.

FRICK: I know, but I mean—some of them must be pretty important people.

LEROY: I wouldn't know. I never kept track of them.

FRICK: You should. Probably some of them must be pretty big. —Never even looked them up?

LEROY: Nope.

FRICK: You realize the importance of Alexander Hamilton, don't you?

LEROY: I know about him, more or less.

FRICK: More or less! He was one of the most important Founding Fathers.

LEROY: I guess so, ya.

FRICK: You read about him, didn't you?

LEROY: Well sure . . . I read about him.

FRICK: Well didn't your father talk about him?

LEROY: Some. But he didn't care for him much.

FRICK: Didn't care for *Alexander Hamilton?*

LEROY: It was something to do with his philosophy. But I never kept
up with the whole thing.

FRICK, *laughing, shaking his head:* Boy, you're quite a character,
aren't you.

*Leroy is silent, reddening. Frick continues chuckling at him for a
moment.*

LEROY: I hope to God your wife is cured, Mr. Frick, I hope she never
has to come back here again.

FRICK, *sensing the hostility:* What have I said?

LEROY: This is the third time in two years for mine, and I don't mean
to be argumentative, but it's got me right at the end of my rope.
For all I know I'm in line for this funny farm myself by now, but I
have to tell you that this could be what's driving so many people
crazy.

FRICK: What is!

LEROY: This.

FRICK: This what?

LEROY: This whole kind of conversation.

FRICK: Why? What's wrong with it?

LEROY: Well never mind.

FRICK: I don't know what you're talking about.

LEROY: Well what's it going to be, equality or what kind of country
—I mean, am I supposed to be ashamed I'm a carpenter?

FRICK: Who said you . . . ?

LEROY: Then why do you talk like this to a man? One minute my altar is terrific and the next minute I'm some kind of shit bucket.

LEROY: Hey now, wait a minute . . . !

LEROY: I don't mean anything against you personally, I know you're a successful man and more power to you, but this whole type of conversation about my clothes—should I be ashamed I'm a carpenter? I mean everybody's talking "labor, labor," how much labor's getting; well if it's so great to be labor how come nobody wants to be it? I mean you ever hear a parent going around saying —*mimes thumb pridefully tucked into suspenders*—"My son is a carpenter"? Do you? Do you ever hear people brag about a bricklayer? I don't know what you are but I'm only a dumb swamp Yankee, but . . . *Suddenly breaks off with a shameful laugh.* Excuse me. I'm really sorry. But you come back here two-three more times and you're liable to start talking the way you were never brought up to. *Opens magazine.*

FRICK: I don't understand what you're so hot about.

LEROY, *looks up from the magazine. Seems to start to explain, then sighs:* Nothing.

He returns to his magazine. Frick shakes his head with a certain condescension, then goes back to the window and looks out.

FRICK: It's one hell of a parking lot, you have to say that for it.

They sit for a long moment in silence, each in his own thoughts.

Blackout.

SCENE TWO

Most of the stage is occupied by Patricia's bedroom. In one of the beds a fully clothed woman lies motionless with one arm over her eyes. She will not move throughout the scene.

Outside this bedroom is a corner of the Recreation Room, bare but for a few scattered chairs.

Presently . . . from just offstage the sound of a Ping-Pong game. The ball comes bouncing into the Recreation Room area and Patricia Hamilton enters chasing it. She captures it and with a sigh of boredom goes offstage with it.

We hear two or three pings and the ball comes onstage again with Patricia Hamilton after it. She starts to return to the game offstage but halts, looks at the ball in her hand, and to someone offstage . . .

PATRICIA: Why are we doing this? Come let's talk, I hate these games.

Mrs. Karen Frick enters. She is in her sixties, very thin, eyeglasses, wispy hair.

I said I'm quitting.

Karen stares at the paddle.

Well never mind. *Studies her watch.* You're very good.

KAREN: My sister-in-law taught me. She used to be a stewardess on the *Queen Mary*. She could even play when the ship was rocking. But she never married.

PATRICIA: Here, put it down, dear.

Karen passively gives up the paddle, then stands there looking uncomfortable.

I'm going to lie down; sit with me, if you like.

KAREN, *indicates Ping-Pong area:* Hardly anyone ever seems to come out there.

PATRICIA: They don't like exercise, they're too depressed.

Patricia lies down. The woman in the other bed does not stir and no attention is paid to her.

Don't feel obliged to say anything if you . . .

KAREN: I get sick to my stomach just looking at a boat. Does your husband hunt?

PATRICIA: Sit down. Relax yourself. You don't have to talk. Although I think you're doing a little better than yesterday.

KAREN: Oh, I like talking with you. *Explaining herself timorously; indicating offstage—and very privately . . .* I should go out—he doesn't like being kept waiting, don't y'know.

PATRICIA: Why are you so afraid? He might start treasuring you more if you make him wait a little. Come, sit.

Karen adventurously sits at the foot of the bed, glancing about nervously.

Men are only big children, you know—give them a chocolate soda every day and pretty soon it doesn't mean a thing to them.

Looks at her watch again. Only reason I'm nervous is that I can't decide whether to go home today. —But you mustn't mention it, will you?

KAREN: Mention . . . ?

PATRICIA: About my pills. I haven't told anybody yet.

Karen looks a bit blank.

Well never mind.

KAREN: Oh! You mean not taking them.

PATRICIA: But you mustn't mention it, will you. The doctor would be very upset.

KAREN: And how long has it been?

PATRICIA: Twenty-one days today. It's the longest I've been clean in maybe fifteen years. I can hardly believe it.

KAREN: Are you Baptist?

PATRICIA: Baptist? No, we're more Methodist. But the church I'd really love hasn't been invented yet.

KAREN, *charmed, slavishly interested:* How would it be?

PATRICIA, *begins to describe it, breaks off:* I can't describe it. *A sign of lostness.* I was raised Lutheran, of course. —But I often go to the Marble Baptist Church on Route 91? I've gotten to like that minister. —You hear what I'm saying, don't you?

Karen looks at her nervously trying to remember.

I must say it's kind of relaxing talking to you, Karen, knowing that you probably won't remember too much. But you'll come out of it all right, you're just a little scared, aren't you. —But who isn't?

Slight pause. Doctor Rockwell is not going to believe I'm doing better without medication but I really think something's clicked inside me. *A deep breath.* I even seem to be breathing easier. And I'm not feeling that sort of fuzziness in my head. —It's like some big bird has been hovering over me for fifteen years, and suddenly it's flown away.

KAREN: I can't stand dead animals, can you?

PATRICIA: Well just insist that he has to stop hunting! You don't have to stand for that, you're a *person.*

KAREN: Well you know, men like to . . .

PATRICIA: Not all—I've known some lovely men. Not many, but a few. This minister I mentioned?—he came one day this summer and sat with me on our porch . . . and we had ice cream and talked for over an hour. You know, when he left his previous church they gave him a Pontiac Grand Am. He made me realize something; he said that I seem to be in like a constant state of prayer. And it's true; every once in a while it stops me short, realizing it. It's like inside me I'm almost continually talking to the Lord. Not in words exactly . . . just—you know—communicating with Him. Or trying to. *Deeply excited, but suppressing it.* I tell you truthfully, if I can really come out of this I'm going to . . . I don't know what . . . fall in love with God. I think I have already.

KAREN: You're really beautiful.

PATRICIA: Oh no, dear, I'm a torn-off rag of my old self. The pills put ten years on my face. If he was a Jew or Italian or even Irish he'd be suing these doctors, but Yankees never sue, you know. Although I have to say the only thing he's been right about is medication.

KAREN: Your husband against pills?

PATRICIA: Fanatical. But of course he can stick his head out the window and go high as a kite on a breath of fresh air. *Looks at her watch.*

KAREN: I really think you're extremely attractive.

PATRICIA: No-no, dear, although I did win the county beauty pageant when I was nineteen. But if you're talking beauty you should have seen my mother. She only died two years ago, age eighty-nine, but I still haven't gotten over it. On the beach, right into her seventies, people would still be staring at her—she had an unbelievable bust right up to the end.

KAREN: I cut this finger once in a broken Coke machine. But we never sued.

PATRICIA: Did your conversation always jump around? Because it could be your pills, believe me; the soul belongs to God, we're not supposed to be stuffing Valium into His mouth.

KAREN: I have a cousin who went right through the windshield and she didn't get a cent. *Slight pause.* And it was five below zero out. *Slight pause.* Her husband's Norwegian.

PATRICIA: Look, dear, I know you're trying but don't feel you have to speak.

KAREN: No, I like speaking to you. Is he Baptist too, your husband?

PATRICIA: I said Methodist. But he's more Episcopal. But he'll go to any church if it's raining. *Slight pause.* I just don't know whether to tell him yet.

KAREN: What.

PATRICIA: That I'm off everything.

KAREN: But he'll like that, won't he?

PATRICIA: Oh yes. But he's going to be doubtful. —Which I am, too, let's face it—who can know for sure that you're going to stay clean? I don't want to fool myself, I've been on one medication or another for almost twenty years. But I do feel a thousand percent better. And I really have no idea how it happened. *Shakes her head.* Dear God, when I think of him hanging in there all these years . . . I'm so ashamed. But at the same time he's absolutely refused to make any money, every one of our children has had to work since they could practically write their names. I can't be expected to applaud, exactly. *Presses her eyes.* I guess sooner or later you just have to stand up and say, "I'm normal, I made it." But it's like standing on top of a stairs and there's no stairs. *Staring ahead.*

KAREN: I think I'd better go out to him. Should I tell your husband you're coming out?

PATRICIA: I think I'll wait a minute.

KAREN, *stands:* He seems very nice.

PATRICIA: —I'll tell you the truth, dear—I've put him through hell and I know it. . . . *Tears threaten her.* I know I have to stop blaming him; it came to me like a visitation two weeks ago, I-must-not-blame-Leroy-anymore. And it's amazing. I lost all desire for medication, I could feel it leaving me like a . . . like a ghost. *Slight pause.* It's just that he's got really well-to-do relatives and he simply will not accept anyone's help. I mean you take the Jews, the Italians, Irish—they've got their Italian-Americans, Irish-Americans, Hispanic-Americans—they stick together and help each other. But you ever hear of Yankee-Americans? Not on your life. Raise his taxes, rob him blind, the Yankee'll just sit there all alone getting sadder and sadder. —But I'm not going to think about it anymore.

KAREN: You have a very beautiful chin.

PATRICIA: Men with half his ability riding around in big expensive cars and now for the second Easter Sunday in a row his rear end collapsed.

KAREN: I think my license must have expired.

PATRICIA, *a surge of deep anger:* I refuse to ride around in a nine-year-old Chevrolet which was bought secondhand in the first place!

KAREN: They say there are only three keys for all General Motors cars. You suppose that's possible?

PATRICIA, *peremptorily now:* Believe me, dear, whatever they tell you, you have got to cut down the medication. It could be what's making your mind jump around . . .

KAREN: No, it's that you mentioned Chevrolet, which is General Motors, you see.

PATRICIA: Oh. . . . Well, let's just forget about it. *Slight pause.* Although you're probably right—here you're carefully locking your car and some crook is walking around with the same keys in his pocket. But everything's a fake, we all know that.

KAREN, *facing Patricia again:* I guess that would be depressing.

PATRICIA: No, that's not what depressed me . . .

KAREN: No, I meant him refusing to amount to anything and then spending money on banjo lessons.

PATRICIA: Did I tell you that?—I keep forgetting what I told you because I never know when you're listening. *Holds out her hand.* Here we go again. *Grasps her hand to stop the shaking.*

KAREN: —You sound like you had a wonderful courtship.

PATRICIA: Oh, Karen, everyone envied us, we were the handsomest pair in town; and I'm not boasting, believe me. *Breaks off; watches her hand shake and covers it again.* I just don't want to have to come back here again, you see. I don't think I could bear that. *Grips her hand, moving about.* I simply have to think positively. But it's unbelievable—he's seriously talking about donating his saw-and-chisel collection to the museum!—some of those tools are as old as the United States, they might be worth a fortune! —But I'm going to look ahead, that's all, just as straight ahead as a highway.

Slight pause.

KAREN: I feel so ashamed.

PATRICIA: For Heaven's sake, why? You've got a right to be depressed. There's more people in hospitals because of depression than any other disease.

KAREN: Is that true?

PATRICIA: Of course! Anybody with any sense has got to be depressed in this country. Unless you're really rich, I suppose. Don't let him shame you, dear.

KAREN: No . . . it's that you have so many thoughts.

PATRICIA: Oh. Well you can have thoughts, too—just remember your soul belongs to God and you mustn't be shoving pills into His mouth.

Slight pause.

KAREN: We're rich, I think.

PATRICIA, *quickly interested:* . . . Really rich?

KAREN: He's got the oil delivery now, and of course he always had the fertilizer and the Chevy dealership, and of course the lumber yard and all. And Isuzus now.

PATRICIA: What's Isuzus?

KAREN: It's a Japanese car.

PATRICIA: . . . I'll just never catch up.

KAREN: We go to Arkansas in the spring.

PATRICIA: Arkansas?

KAREN: For the catfish. It's where I broke down. But I can't help it, the sight of catfish makes me want to vomit. Not that I was trying to . . . you know . . . do anything. I just read the instructions on the bottle wrong. Do you mind if I ask you something?

PATRICIA: I hope it's nothing personal, is it?

KAREN: Well I don't know.

PATRICIA: . . . Well go ahead, what is it?

KAREN: Do you shop in the A&P or Stop & Shop?

PATRICIA: . . . I'm wondering if you've got the wrong medication. But I guess you'll never overdose—you vomit at the drop of a hat. It may be your secret blessing.

KAREN: —He wants to get me out of the house more, but it's hard to make up my mind where.

PATRICIA: Well . . . A&P is good. Or Stop & Shop. More or less. Kroger's is good for fish sometimes.

KAREN: Which do you like best? I'll go where you go.

PATRICIA: You're very flattering. *Stands, inner excitement.* It's amazing —I'm really beginning to feel wonderful; maybe I ought to go home with him today. I mean what does it come down to, really? —it's simply a question of confidence . . .

KAREN: I wish we could raise some vegetables like we did on the farm. Do you?

PATRICIA: Oh, he raises things in our yard. Healthy things like salsify and collards—and kale. You ever eat kale?

KAREN: I can't remember kale.

PATRICIA: You might as well salt your shower curtain and chop it up with a tomato.

KAREN: —So . . . meats are . . . which?—A&P?

PATRICIA: No. Meats are Stop & Shop. I'm really thinking I might go home today. It's just not his fault, I have to remember that . . .

KAREN: But staples?

PATRICIA: What? —Oh. Stop & Shop.

KAREN: Then what's for A&P?

PATRICIA: Vegetables.

KAREN: Oh right. And Kroger's?

PATRICIA: Why don't you just forget Kroger's.

KAREN, *holds up five fingers, bends one at a time:* . . . Then Stop & Shop . . .

PATRICIA: Maybe it's that you're trying to remember three things. Whyn't you just do A&P and Stop & Shop.

Slight pause.

KAREN: I kind of liked Kroger's.

PATRICIA: Then go to Kroger's, for Heaven's sake!

KAREN: Well I guess I'll go out to him. *Moves to go. Halts.* I hope you aren't really leaving today, are you?

PATRICIA, *higher tension:* I'm deciding.

KAREN: Well . . . here I go, I guess. *Halts again.* I meant to tell you, I kind of like the banjo. It's very good with tap dancing.

PATRICIA: Tap dancing.

KAREN: There's a tap teacher lives on our road.

PATRICIA: You tap-dance?

KAREN: Well John rented a video of Ginger Rogers and Fred Astaire, and I kind of liked it. I can sing "Cheek to Cheek"? Would you like to hear it?

PATRICIA: Sure, go ahead—this is certainly a surprise.

KAREN, *sings in a frail voice:* "Heaven, I'm in heaven, and the cares that clung around me through the week . . ."

PATRICIA: That's beautiful, Karen! Listen, what exactly does Doctor Rockwell say about you?

KAREN: Well, he says it's quite common when a woman is home alone all day.

PATRICIA: What's common?

KAREN: Something moving around in the next room?

PATRICIA: Oh, I see. —You have any idea who it is?

KAREN: My mother. —My husband might bring my tap shoes and tails . . . but he probably forgot. I have a high hat and shorts too. And a walking stick? But would they allow dancing in here?

PATRICIA: They might. But of course the minute they see you enjoying yourself they'll probably try to knock you out with a pill.

Karen makes to go, halts again.

KAREN: Did your mother like you?

PATRICIA: Oh yes. We were all very close. Didn't yours?

KAREN: No. She left the whole farm to her cousin. Tell about your family, can you? Were they really all blond?

PATRICIA: Oh as blond as the tassels on Golden Bantam corn . . . everybody'd turn and look when we went by. My mother was perfection. We all were, I guess. *With a chuckle.* You know, we had a flat roof extending from the house over the garage, and mother and my sisters and me—on the first warm spring days we used to sunbathe out there.

KAREN, *covering her mouth:* No! You mean nude?

PATRICIA: Nudity doesn't matter that much in Sweden, and we were all brought up to love the sun. And we'd near die laughing because the minute we dropped our robes—you know how quiet a town Grenville is—you could hear the footsteps going up the clock tower over the Presbyterian church, and we pretended not to notice but that little narrow tower was just packed with Presbyterians.

KAREN: Good lord!

PATRICIA: We'd stretch out and pretend not to see a thing. And then my mother'd sit up suddenly and point up at the steeple and yell, "Boo!" And they'd all go running down the stairs like mice!

They both enjoy the laugh.

KAREN: I think your husband's very good-looking, isn't he.

PATRICIA: He is, but my brothers . . . I mean the way they stood, and walked . . . and their teeth! Charles won the All-New England golf tournament, and Buzz came within a tenth of an inch of the gold medal in the pole vault—that was in the Portugal Olympics.

KAREN: My! Do you still get together much?

PATRICIA: Oh, they're all gone now.

KAREN: Moved away?

PATRICIA: No . . . dead.

KAREN: Oh my. They overstrain?

PATRICIA: Buzz hung himself on his wife's closet door.

KAREN: Oh my!

PATRICIA: Eight days later Charles shot himself on the tractor.

KAREN, *softly:* Oh my. Did they leave a note or anything?

PATRICIA: No. But we all knew what it was.

KAREN: Can you say?

PATRICIA: Disappointment. We were all brought up expecting to be wonderful, and . . . *breaks off with a shrug* . . . just wasn't.

KAREN: Well . . . here I go.

Karen exits. Patricia stares ahead for a moment in a blankly reminiscent mood. Now she looks at her face in a mirror, smoothing wrinkles away . . .

Leroy enters.

PATRICIA: I was just coming out.

LEROY: 'Cause Mrs. Frick . . .

PATRICIA, *cuts him off by drawing his head down and stroking his cheek. And in a soft but faintly patronizing tone:* . . . I was just coming out, Leroy. You don't have to repeat everything. Come, sit with me and let's not argue.

LEROY: . . . How's your day been?

She is still moved by her brothers' memory; also, she hasn't received something she hoped for from him. She shrugs and turns her head away.

PATRICIA: I've had worse.

LEROY: Did you wash your hair?

PATRICIA, *pleased he noticed:* How can you tell?

LEROY: Looks livelier. Is that nail polish?

PATRICIA: M-hm.

LEROY: Good. You're looking good, Patty.

PATRICIA: I'm feeling better. Not completely but a lot.

LEROY, *nods approvingly:* Great! Did he change your medication or something?

PATRICIA: No.

LEROY: Something different about you.

PATRICIA, *mysteriously excited:* You think so?

LEROY: Your eyes are clearer. You seem more like you're . . . connecting.

PATRICIA: I am, I think. But I warn you, I'm nervous.

LEROY: That's okay. Your color is more . . . I don't know . . . vigorous.

PATRICIA: Is it? *She touches her face.*

LEROY: You look almost like years ago . . .

PATRICIA: Something's happened but I don't want to talk about it yet.

LEROY: Really? Like what?

PATRICIA, *instant resistance:* I just said I . . .

LEROY: . . . Okay. *Goes to a window.* —It looks like rain outside, but we can walk around if you like. They've got a beautiful tulip bed down there; the colors really shine in this gray light. Reds and purple and whites, and a gray. Never saw a tulip be that kind of gray.

PATRICIA: How's Amelia's leg? Are you getting her to change her bandage?

LEROY: Yes. But she'd better stop thinking she can drive a car.

PATRICIA: Well, why don't you tell her?

LEROY, *a little laugh:* That'll be the day, won't it, when she starts listening to her father.

PATRICIA, *a softness despite her language:* She might if you laid down the law without just complaining. And if she could hear something besides disappointment in your voice.

LEROY: She's learned to look down at me, Patty, you know that.

PATRICIA, *strongly, but nearly a threat of weeping:* Well, I hope you're not blaming me for that.

LEROY, *he holds back, stands silent. Then puffs out his cheeks and blows, shaking his head with a defensive grin:* Not my day, I see.

PATRICIA: Maybe it could have been.

LEROY: I was looking forward to telling you something.

PATRICIA: What.

LEROY: I got Harrelson to agree to twelve-thousand-five for the altar.

PATRICIA: There, you see!—and you were so glad to accept eight. I told you . . . !

LEROY: I give you all the credit. I finally got it through my thick skull, I said to myself, okay, you are slower than most, but quality's got a right to be slow. And he didn't make a peep—twelve thousand, five hundred dollars.

She looks at him, immensely sad.

—Well why do you look so sad?

PATRICIA: Come here. *Draws him down, kisses him.* I'm glad. . . . I just couldn't help thinking of all these years wasted trying to get you to charge enough; but I've decided to keep looking straight ahead, not back—I'm very glad you got the twelve. You've done a wonderful thing.

LEROY, *excited:* Listen, what has he got you on?

PATRICIA: Well, I'm still a long way from perfect, but I . . .

LEROY: Patty, nothing's perfect except a hot bath.

PATRICIA: It's nothing to joke about. I told you I'm nervous, I'm not used to . . . to . . .

LEROY: He changed your medication, didn't he.

PATRICIA: I just don't want you to think I have no problems anymore.

LEROY: Oh, I'd never think that, Patty. Has he put you on something new?

PATRICIA: *He* hasn't done anything.

Pause.

LEROY: Okay, I'll shut up.

She sweeps her hair back; he silently observes her. Then . . .

. . . This Mr. Frick handles oil burners; I don't know if I can trust him but he says he'd give me a good buy. We could use a new burner.

PATRICIA: What would you say if I said I'm thinking of coming home.

LEROY, *a pause filled with doubt:* You are? When?

PATRICIA: Maybe next Thursday. For good.

LEROY: Uh huh.

PATRICIA: You don't sound very positive.

LEROY: You know you're the only one can make that decision, Pat. You want to come home I'm always happy to take you home.

Slight pause.

PATRICIA: I feel if I could look ahead just the right amount I'd be all right.

LEROY: What do you mean?

PATRICIA: I realized something lately; when I'm home I have a tendency—especially in the afternoons when everybody's out and I'm alone—I look very far ahead. What I should do is only look ahead a little bit, like to the evening or the next day. And then it's all right. It's when I start looking years ahead . . . *slight pause* . . . You once told me why you think I got sick. I've forgotten . . . what did you say?

LEROY: What do I really know about it, Pat?

PATRICIA: Why do you keep putting yourself down?—you've got to stop imitating your father. There are things you know very well. —Remind me what you said . . . Why am I sick?

LEROY: I always thought it was your family.

PATRICIA, *fingers pressing on her eyes:* I want to concentrate. Go on.

LEROY: They were so close, they were all over each other, and you all had this—you know—very high opinion of yourselves; each and every one of you was automatically going to go to the head of the line just because your name was Sorgenson. And life isn't that way, so you got sick.

Long pause; she stares, nodding.

PATRICIA: You've had no life at all, have you.

LEROY: I wouldn't say that.

PATRICIA: I can't understand how I never saw it.

LEROY: Why?—it's been great watching the kids growing up; and I've had some jobs I've enjoyed . . .

PATRICIA: But not your wife.

LEROY: It's a long time since I blamed you, Pat. It's your upbringing.

LEROY: Well I could blame yours too, couldn't I.

LEROY: You sure could.

PATRICIA: I mean this constant optimism is very irritating when you're fifty times more depressed than I am.

LEROY: Now Patty, you know that's not . . .

PATRICIA: You are depressed, Leroy! Because you're scared of people, you really don't trust anyone, and that's incidentally why you never made any money. You could have set the world on fire but you can't bear to work along with other human beings.

LEROY: The last human being I took on to help me tried to steal my half-inch Stanley chisel.

PATRICIA: You mean you *think* he tried . . .

LEROY: I didn't think anything, I found it in his tool box. And that's an original Stanley, not the junk they sell today.

PATRICIA: So what!

LEROY: So what?—that man has three grandchildren! And he's a Chapman—that's one of the oldest upstanding families in the county.

PATRICIA, *emphatically, her point proved:* Which is why you're depressed.

LEROY, *laughs:* I'm not, but why shouldn't I be?—a Chapman stealing a chisel? I mean God Almighty, they've had generals in that family, secretaries of state or some goddam thing. Anyway, if I'm depressed it's from something that happened, not something I imagine.

PATRICIA: I feel like a log that keeps bumping against another log in the middle of the river.

LEROY: Boy, you're a real roller coaster. We were doing great there for a minute, what got us off on this?

PATRICIA: I can't be at peace when I know you are full of denial, and that's saying it straight.

LEROY: What denial? *Laughs.* You want me to say I'm a failure?

PATRICIA: That is not what I . . .

LEROY: Hey, I know what—I'll get a bumper sticker printed up— "The driver of this car is a failure!" —I betcha I could sell a hundred million of them . . . *A sudden fury:* . . . Or maybe I should just drive out on a tractor and shoot myself!

PATRICIA: That's a terrible thing to say to me, Leroy!

LEROY: Well I'm sorry, Patty, but I'm not as dumb as I look—I'm never going to win if I have to compete against your brothers!

PATRICIA, *chastened for the moment:* I did not say you're a failure.

LEROY: I didn't mean to yell; I'm sorry. I know you don't mean to sound like you do, sometimes.

PATRICIA, *unable to retrieve:* I said nothing about a failure. *On the verge of weeping.*

LEROY: It's okay, maybe I am a failure; but in my opinion no more than the rest of this country.

PATRICIA: What happened?—I thought this visit started off so nicely.

LEROY: Maybe you're not used to being so alert; you've been so lethargic for a long time, you know.

She moves; he watches her.

I'm sure of it, Pat, if you could only find two ounces of trust I know we could still have a life.

PATRICIA: I know. *Slight pause; she fights down tears.* What did you have in mind, exactly, when you said it was my upbringing?

LEROY: I don't know . . . I had a flash of your father, that time long ago when we were sitting on your porch . . . we were getting things ready for our wedding . . . and right in front of you he turns to me cool as a cucumber and says—*through laughter, mimicking Swedish accent*—"No Yankee will ever be good enough for a Swedish girl." I nearly fell off into the rosebushes.

PATRICIA, *laughs with a certain delight:* Well, he was old-fashioned . . .

LEROY, *laughing:* Yeah, a real old-fashioned welcome into the family!

PATRICIA: Well, the Yankees *were* terrible to us.

LEROY: That's a hundred years ago, Pat.

PATRICIA, *starting to anger:* You shouldn't keep denying this! —They paid them fifty cents a week and called us dumb Swedes with strong backs and weak minds and did nothing but make us ridiculous.

LEROY: But, Patty, if you walk around town today there isn't a good piece of property that isn't owned by Swedes.

PATRICIA: But that's now.

LEROY: Well when are we living?

PATRICIA: We were treated like animals, some Yankee doctors wouldn't come out to a Swedish home to deliver a baby . . .

LEROY, *laughs:* Well all I hope is that I'm the last Yankee so people can start living today instead of a hundred years ago.

PATRICIA: There was something else you said. About standing on line.

LEROY: On line?

PATRICIA: That you'll always be at the head of the line because . . . *breaks off.*

LEROY: I'm the only one on it.

PATRICIA: . . . Is that really true? You do compete, don't you? You must, at least in your mind?

LEROY: Only with myself. We're really all on a one-person line, Pat. I learned that in these years.

Pause. She stares ahead.

PATRICIA: That's very beautiful. Where'd you get that idea?

LEROY: I guess I made it up, I don't know. It's up to you, Pat—if you feel you're ready, let's go home. Now or Thursday or whenever. What about medication?

PATRICIA, *makes herself ready:* I wasn't going to tell you for another week or two, till I'm absolutely rock sure; —I've stopped taking anything for . . . this is twenty-one days.

LEROY: *Anything?*

She nods with a certain suspense.

My God, Patty. And you feel all right?

PATRICIA: . . . I haven't felt this way in—fifteen years. I've no idea why, but I forgot to take anything, and I slept right through till morning, and I woke up and it was like . . . I'd been blessed during the night. And I haven't had anything since.

LEROY: Did I tell you or didn't I!

PATRICIA: But it's different for you. You're not addictive . . .

LEROY: But didn't I tell you all that stuff is poison? I'm just flying, Patty.

PATRICIA, *clasps her hands to steady herself:* But I'm afraid about coming home. I don't know if I'm jumping the gun. I *feel* I could, but . . .

LEROY: Well, let's talk about it. Is it a question of trusting yourself? Because I think if you've come this far . . .

PATRICIA: Be quiet a minute! *She holds his hand.* Why have you stayed with me?

LEROY, *laughs:* God knows!

PATRICIA: I've been very bad to you sometimes, Leroy, I really see that now. *Starting to weep.* Tell me the truth; in all these years, have you gone to other women? I wouldn't blame you, I just want to know.

LEROY: Well I've thought of it but I never did anything.

PATRICIA, *looking deeply into his eyes:* You really haven't, have you.

LEROY: No.

PATRICIA: Why?

LEROY: I just kept hoping you'd come out of this.

PATRICIA: But it's been so long.

LEROY: I know.

PATRICIA: Even when I'd . . . throw things at you?

LEROY: Uh uh.

PATRICIA: Like that time with the roast?

LEROY: Well, that's one time I came pretty close. But I knew it was those damned pills, not you.

PATRICIA: But why would you be gone night after night? That was a woman, wasn't it.

LEROY: No. Some nights I went over to the library basement to practice banjo with Phil Palumbo. Or to Manny's Diner for some donuts and talk to the fellas.

PATRICIA, *slightest tinge of suspicion:* There are fellas there at *night?*

LEROY: Sure; working guys, mostly young single fellas. But some with wives. You know—have a beer, watch TV.

PATRICIA: And women?

LEROY, *a short beat:* —You know, Pat—and I'm not criticizing—but wouldn't it be better for you to try believing a person instead of trying not to believe?

PATRICIA: I'm just wondering if you know . . . there's lots of women would love having you. But you probably don't know that, do you.

LEROY: Sure I do.

PATRICIA: You know lots of women would love to have you?

LEROY: . . . Well, yes, I know that.

PATRICIA: Really. How do you know that?

LEROY, *his quick, open laugh:* I can tell.

PATRICIA: Then what's keeping you? Why don't you move out?

LEROY: Pat, you're torturing me.

PATRICIA: I'm trying to find myself!

She moves in stress, warding off an explosion. There is angry resentment in his voice.

LEROY: I'd remember you happy and loving—that's what kept me; as long ago as that is now, I'd remember how you'd pull on your stockings and get a little makeup on and pin up your hair. . . . When you're positive about life there's just nobody like you. Nobody. Not in life, not in the movies, not on TV. *Slight pause.* But I'm not going to deny it—if it wasn't for the kids I probably *would* have gone.

She is silent, but loaded with something unspoken.

You're wanting to tell me something, aren't you.

PATRICIA: . . . I know what a lucky woman I've been.

LEROY, *he observes her:* —What is it, you want me to stop coming to see you for a while? Please tell me, Pat; there's something on your mind.

Pause. She forces it out.

PATRICIA: I know I shouldn't feel this way, but I'm not too sure I could stand it, knowing that it's never going to . . . I mean, will it ever change anymore?

LEROY: You mean—is it ever going to be "wonderful."

She looks at him, estimating.

Well—no, I guess this is pretty much it; although to me it's already wonderful—I mean the kids, and there are some clear New England mornings when you want to drink the air and the sunshine.

PATRICIA: You can make more out of a change in temperature than any human being I ever heard of—I can't live on weather!

LEROY: Pat, we're getting old! This is just about as rich and handsome as I'm ever going to be and as good as you're ever going to look, so you want to be with me or not?

PATRICIA: I don't want to fool either of us . . . I can't bear it when you can't pay the bills . . .

LEROY: But I'm a carpenter—this is probably the way it's been for carpenters since they built Noah's ark. What do you want to do?

PATRICIA: I'm honestly not sure I could hold up. Not when I hear your sadness all the time and your eyes are full of disappointment. You seem . . . *breaks off.*

LEROY: . . . How do I seem?

PATRICIA: I shouldn't say it.

LEROY: . . . Beaten. Like it's all gone by. *Hurt, but holding on:* All right, Patty, then I might as well say it—I don't think you *ever* had a medical problem; you have an attitude problem . . .

PATRICIA: My problem is spiritual.

LEROY: Okay, I don't mind calling it spiritual.

PATRICIA: Well that's a new note; I thought these ministers were all quacks.

LEROY: Not all; but the ones who make house calls with women, eating up all the ice cream, are not my idea of spiritual.

PATRICIA: *You* know what spiritual is?

LEROY: For me? Sure. Ice skating.

PATRICIA: Ice skating is spiritual.

LEROY: Yes, and skiing! To me spiritual is whatever makes me forget myself and feel happy to be alive. Like even a well-sharpened saw, or a perfect compound joint.

PATRICIA: Maybe this is why we can't get along—spiritual is nothing you can see, Leroy.

LEROY: Really! Then why didn't God make everything invisible! We are in this world and you're going to have to find some way to love it!

Her eyes are filling with tears.

Pounding on me is not going to change anything to wonderful, Patty.

She seems to be receiving him.

I'll say it again, because it's the only thing that's kept me from going crazy—you just have to love this world. *He comes to her, takes her hand.* Come home. Maybe it'll take a while, but I really believe you can make it.

Uncertainty filling her face . . .

All right, don't decide now, I'll come back Thursday and we'll see then.

PATRICIA: Where you going now?

LEROY: For my banjo lesson. I'm learning a new number. —I'll play it for you if you want to hear it.

PATRICIA, *hesitates, then kisses him:* Couldn't you do it on guitar?

LEROY: It's not the same on guitar. *He goes to his banjo case and opens it.*

PATRICIA: But banjo sounds so picky.

LEROY: But that's what's good about it, it's clean, like a toothpick . . .

Enter the Fricks.

LEROY: Oh hi, Mrs. Frick.

KAREN: He brought my costume. Would you care to see it? *To Frick:* This is her—Mrs. Hamilton.

FRICK: Oh! How do you do?

KAREN: This is my husband.

PATRICIA: How do you do?

FRICK: She's been telling me all about you. *Shaking Patricia's hand:* I want to say that I'm thankful to you.

PATRICIA: Really? What for?

FRICK: Well what she says you've been telling her. About her attitude and all.

KAREN, *to Patricia:* Would you like to see my costume? I also have a blue one, but . . .

FRICK, *overriding her:* . . . By the way, I'm Frick Lumber, I recognized your husband right away . . .

KAREN: Should I put it on?

PATRICIA: Sure, put it on!

Leroy starts tuning his banjo.

FRICK, *to Patricia:* All it is is a high hat and shorts, y'know . . . nothing much to it.

KAREN, *to Frick:* Shouldn't I?

PATRICIA: Why not, for Heaven's sake?

FRICK: Go ahead, if they want to see it. *Laughs to Patricia.* She found it in a catalogue. I think it's kinda silly at her age, but I admit I'm a conservative kind of person . . .

KAREN, *cutting him off, deeply embarrassed:* I'll only be a minute. *She starts out, and stops, and to Patricia:* You really think I should?

PATRICIA: Of course!

FRICK, *suppressing an angry embarrassment:* Karen, honey, if you're going to do it, do it.

Karen exits with valise. Leroy tunes his instrument.

FRICK: The slightest decision, she's got to worry it into the ground. —But I have to tell you, it's years since I've seen this much life in her, she's like day and night. What exactly'd you say to her? *To Leroy, thumbing toward Patricia:* She says she just opened up her eyes . . .

LEROY, *surprised:* Patricia?

FRICK: I have to admit, it took me a while to realize it's a sickness . . .

PATRICIA: You're not the only one.

FRICK: Looked to me like she was just favoring herself; I mean the woman has everything, what right has she got to start shooting blanks like that? I happen to be a great believer in self-discipline, started from way down below sea level myself, sixty acres of rocks and swampland is all we had. That's why I'm so glad that somebody's talked to her with your attitude.

PATRICIA, *vamping for time:* What . . . what attitude do you mean?

FRICK: Just that you're so . . . so positive.

Leroy looks up at Patricia, thunderstruck.

She says you made her realize all the things she could be doing instead of mooning around all day . . .

PATRICIA: Well I think being positive is the only way.

FRICK: That's just what I tell her . . .

PATRICIA: But you have to be careful not to sound so disappointed in her.

FRICK: I sound disappointed?

PATRICIA: In a way, I think. —She's got to feel treasured, you see.

FRICK: I appreciate that, but the woman can stand in one place for half an hour at a time practically without moving.

PATRICIA: Well that's the sickness, you see.

FRICK: I realize that. But she won't even go shopping . . .

PATRICIA: You see? You're sounding disappointed in her.

FRICK, *angering:* I am not disappointed in her! I'm just telling you the situation!

PATRICIA: Mr. Frick, she's standing under a mountain a mile high— you've got to help her over it. That woman has very big possibilities!

FRICK: Think so.

PATRICIA: Absolutely.

FRICK: I hope you're right. *To Leroy, indicating Patricia:* You don't mind my saying it, you could do with a little of her optimism.

LEROY, *turns from Patricia, astonished.* Huh?

FRICK, *to Patricia, warmly:* Y'know, she made me have a little platform built down the cellar, with a big full-length mirror so she could see herself dance . . .

PATRICIA: But do you spend time watching her . . .

FRICK: Well she says not to till she's good at it.

PATRICIA: That's because she's terrified of your criticism.

FRICK: But I haven't made any criticism.

PATRICIA: But do you like tap dancing?

FRICK: Well I don't know, I never thought about it one way or another.

PATRICIA: Well that's the thing, you see. It happens to mean a great deal to her . . .

FRICK: I'm for it, I don't mean I'm not for it. But don't tell me you think it's normal for a woman her age to be getting out of bed two, three in the morning and start practicing.

PATRICIA: Well maybe she's trying to get you interested in it. Are you?

FRICK: In tap dancing? Truthfully, no.

PATRICIA: Well there you go . . .

FRICK: Well we've got a lot of new competition in our fuel-oil business . . .

PATRICIA: Fuel oil!

FRICK: I've got seven trucks on the road that I've got to keep busy . . .

PATRICIA: Well there you go, maybe that's why your wife is in here.

FRICK, *visibly angering:* Well I can't be waked up at two o'clock in the morning and be any good next day, now can I. She's not normal.

PATRICIA: Normal! They've got whole universities debating what's normal. Who knows what's normal, Mr. Frick?

FRICK: You mean getting out of bed at two o'clock in the morning and putting on a pair of tap shoes is a common occurrence in this country? I don't think so. —But I didn't mean to argue when you're . . . not feeling well.

PATRICIA: I've never felt better.

She turns away, and Frick looks with bewildered surprise to Leroy, who returns him a look of suppressed laughter.

FRICK: Well you sure know how to turn somebody inside out.

Karen enters; she is dressed in satin shorts, a tailcoat, a high hat, tap shoes, and as they turn to look at her, she pulls out a collapsible walking stick, and strikes a theatrical pose.

PATRICIA: Well now, don't you look great!

KAREN, *desperate for reassurance:* You really like it?

LEROY: That looks terrific!

PATRICIA: Do a step!

KAREN: I don't have my tape. *Turns to Frick, timorously:* But if you'd sing "Swanee River . . ."

FRICK: Oh Karen, for God's sake!

PATRICIA: I can sing it . . .

KAREN: He knows my speed. Please, John . . . just for a minute.

FRICK: All right, go ahead. *Unhappily, he sings:* "Way down upon the Swanee River . . ."

KAREN: Wait, you're too fast . . .

FRICK, *slower and angering:* "Way—down—upon—the—Swanee River,
Far, far away.
That's where my heart is turning ever . . ."
[*etc.*]

Karen taps out her number, laboriously but for a short stretch with a promise of grace. Frick continues singing . . .

PATRICIA: Isn't she wonderful?

LEROY: Hey, she's great!

Karen dances a bit more boldly, a joyous freedom starting into her.

PATRICIA: She's marvelous! Look at her, Mr. Frick!

A hint of the sensuous in Karen now; Frick, embarrassed, uneasily avoids more than a glance at his wife.

FRICK: ". . . everywhere I roam . . ."

PATRICIA: Will you look at her!

FRICK, *hard-pressed, explodes:* I am looking at her, goddammit!

This astonishing furious shout, his reddened face, stops everything. A look of fear is on Karen's face.

KAREN, *apologetically to Patricia:* He *was* looking at me . . . *To Frick:* She didn't mean you *weren't* looking, she meant . . .

FRICK, *rigidly repressing his anger and embarrassment:* I've got to run along now.

KAREN: I'm so sorry, John, but she . . .

FRICK, *rigidly:* Nothing to be sorry about, dear. Very nice to have met you folks.

He starts to exit. Karen moves to intercept him.

KAREN: Oh John, I hope you're not . . . [going to be angry.]

JOHN: I'm just fine. *He sees her despair coming on.* What are you looking so sad about?—you danced great . . .

She is immobile.

I'm sorry to've raised my voice but it don't mean I'm disappointed, dear. You understand? *A nervous glance toward Patricia.*

Stiffly, with enormous effort: . . . You . . . you danced better than I ever saw you.

She doesn't change.

Now look here, Karen, I hope you don't feel I'm . . . disappointed or something, you hear . . . ? 'Cause I'm not. And that's definite.

She keeps staring at him.

I'll try to make it again on Friday. —Keep it up.

He abruptly turns and exits.

Karen stands perfectly still, staring at nothing.

PATRICIA: Karen?

Karen seems not to hear, standing there facing the empty door in her high hat and costume.

How about Leroy playing it for you? *To Leroy:* Play it.

LEROY: I could on the guitar, but I never did on this . . .

PATRICIA: Well couldn't you try it?—I don't know what good that thing is.

LEROY: Well here . . . let me see.

He picks out "Swanee River" on his banjo, but Karen doesn't move.

PATRICIA: There you go, Karen! Try it, I love your dancing! Come on . . . *Sings:* "Way down upon the Swanee river . . ."

Karen now breaks her motionlessly depressed mode and looks at Patricia. Leroy continues playing, humming along with it. His picking is getting more accurate . . .

PATRICIA: Is it the right tempo? Tell him!

KAREN, *very very softly:* Could you play a little faster?

Leroy speeds it up. With an unrelieved sadness, Karen goes into her number, does a few steps, but stops. Leroy gradually stops playing. Karen walks out. Patricia starts to follow her but gives it up and comes to a halt.

Leroy turns to Patricia, who is staring ahead. Now she turns to Leroy.

He meets her gaze, his face filled with inquiry. He comes to her and stands there.

For a long moment neither of them moves. Then she reaches out and touches his face—there is a muted gratitude in her gesture.

She goes to a closet and takes a small overnight bag to the bed and puts her things into it.

Leroy watches her for a moment, then stows his banjo in its case, and stands waiting for her. She starts to put on a light coat. He comes and helps her into it.

Her face is charged with her struggle against her self-doubt.

LEROY, *laughs, but about to weep:* Ready?

PATRICIA, *filling up:* Leroy . . .

LEROY: One day at a time, Pat—you're already twenty-one ahead. Kids are going to be so happy to have you home.

PATRICIA: I can't believe it. . . . I've had nothing.

LEROY: It's a miracle.

PATRICIA: Thank you. *Breaking through her own resistance, she draws him to her and kisses him. Grinning tauntingly:* . . . That car going to get us home?

LEROY, *laughs:* Stop picking on that car, it's all checked out!

They start toward the door, he carrying her bag and his banjo.

PATRICIA: Once you believe in something you just never know when to stop, do you.

LEROY: Well there's very little rust, and the new ones aren't half as well built . . .

PATRICIA: Waste not, want not.

LEROY: Well I really don't *go* for those new Chevies . . .

She walks out, he behind her. Their voices are heard . . .

PATRICIA: Between the banjo and that car I've certainly got a whole lot to look forward to.

His laughter sounds down the corridor.

The woman on the bed stirs, then falls back and remains motionless. A stillness envelops the whole stage.

END.

ABOUT THEATRE LANGUAGE

I

When I began writing plays in the late thirties, something called realism was the undisputed reigning style in the American commercial theatre—which was just about all the theatre there was in this country. The same was more or less the case in Britain. If not a mass art, theatre then could still be thought of at least as a popular one, although everyone knew—long before television—that something of its common appeal had gone out of it, and a lot of its twenties' glamour, too. One blamed the movies, which had stolen so much of the audience and thus theatre's old dominance as a cultural influence. Notwithstanding the obvious fact that the audience was predominantly middle class, we continued to imagine that we were making plays for people of many different educational and cultural levels, a representative variety of the city and even the country. If this was never really true, there was certainly no thought of appealing to a clique of college graduates or to academics and their standards. A *New York Times* critic like George S. Kaufman had both feet in show business and became the most popular writer of comedies of the period, while Brooks Atkinson may have had one eye on Aristotle but understood that his readers were Americans impatient with any theatrical enterprise that required either education or patience. Outside New York there were at least the remains of the twenties' touring wheel, theatres in many smaller cities regularly attended by quite ordinary citizens eager for last year's Broadway hits, albeit with replacement casts. In New York, with a ticket price of fifty-five cents to four dollars and forty cents, one somehow took for granted that a professor might be sitting next to a housewife, a priest beside a skilled worker or perhaps a grammar-school teacher, a small or large business executive beside a student. This conception of the demotic audience, accurate or not, influenced the writing of plays directed at the commonsensical experience of everyday people. Missing were black or Asian or Hispanic faces, of course, but they were beyond the consciousness of the prevailing culture. As for production costs, even into the forties they were within reason; plays like *All My Sons* or *Death of a Salesman,* for example, cost between twenty and forty thousand to produce, a budget small enough to be raised by half a dozen modest contributors, who might lose all, with some embarrassment but reasonably little pain, or make a killing.

Radicals—people like myself, trying to convince ourselves that we were carrying on the age-old tradition of theatre as a civic art rather than a purely commercial one—were in a conflict; to attract even the fitful interest of a Broadway producer, and subsequently to engage the audience, we had to bow to realism, even if the poetic forms were what we really admired or at least wished to explore. An Expressionist like the German Ernst Toller, for example, would not have been read past his sixth page by a Broadway producer or, for that matter, one in London. Among the playwrights one thinks of as important, not one was—or is now—welcome in the commercial theatre. Not Chekhov, not Ibsen, not Hauptmann, not Pirandello, Strindberg, Turgenev—not even Shaw. To so much as think of performing a Beckett play like *Waiting for Godot* in the general proximity of Broadway a cast of movie stars and a short run are essential— Lincoln Center pulled it off in 1988—and things were probably a bit worse half a century ago. One need only read O'Neill's letters of complaint at the "showshop" of Broadway and the narrow compass of the American audience's imagination—or in Britain, Shaw's ridicule of his countrymen's provincialism—to understand the problem; for some mysterious reason the Anglo-Saxon culture regarded theatre as an entertainment first and last, an art of escape with none of the Continental or Russian interest in moral and philosophical opportunities or obligations. Very occasionally in America there was an *Adding Machine* by the young Elmer Rice, but such a breakout from conventional realism was rare enough to be brought up in conversation for years after, like a calf born with five legs. The English-language theatre was pridefully commercial, a profit-making enterprise which wed it to a form whose surfaces of familiar reality would be universally recognized. Captain Shotover's outcry, "I like to know where I am!" could have been sewn to the flag of this theatre. Only musicals had the happy license to stretch reality, at least to some extent. But for straight plays, even satire was too strange to prosper; George Kaufman defined satire as what closes on Saturday night.

The point here is that what we think of as "straight realism" was tiresome half a century ago, indeed longer ago than that, but it was accepted by the audiences and almost all the reviewers as a reflection of life. Nonetheless it should be remembered that realism has reemerged at various moments to very capably express the essence of an era. At a time when "experimental" is all the virtue a play needs in order to gain serious consideration, it is not a bad idea to confess that an extraordinarily few such researches have achieved any kind of enduring life. It is not quite enough to know how to escape; one has also to think of arriving somewhere.

In the thirties, probably the single exception—at least that I was aware of—to realism's domination was the WPA's *Living Newspaper*, the one formal innovation of American theatre. An epic in more or less presentational form, written like movies by groups of writers, rather than individually, it dealt in an overtly exuberant spirit with social issues like public ownership of electrical power, labor unions, agriculture, and medicine, and was extremely popular. Significantly, the WPA was government-subsidized, and did not have to make a profit. Using unemployed actors, designers, technicians, a show could call upon large casts and elaborate scenery and production elements. And the ticket was low-priced. The WPA could send Orson Welles, for example, into Harlem storefronts with a big cast playing *Doctor Faustus*, charging a quarter a seat. But theatre-for-profit was hardly affected by what might be called this epic-populist approach—it was simply too expensive to produce.

I mention these mundane matters because they profoundly affect style in the theatre, which, like politics, is always the art of the possible.

There were at least a dozen playwrights regularly feeding the commercial theatre in the years before World War II, and all but perhaps Odets and Hellman would have pridefully declared that their sole purpose was to entertain. Those playwrights were sophisticated and no doubt knew all about the Continental theatre tradition, and its aspiring to the philosophical condition, something like that of the Greeks or, in a different way, the Elizabethans. The Theatre Guild, for one, had been started in the twenties in part to bring that kind of theatre to America, the theatre of Pirandello, Schnitzler, Ibsen, and Strindberg.

In the thirties, one American styled himself a political revolutionary, and that was Clifford Odets. O'Neill, of course, had been the aesthetic rebel but his socialism was private rather than informing his plays, although *The Hairy Ape* is surely an anticapitalist work. It was his formal experiments and tragic mood that set him apart. O'Neill was a totally isolated phenomenon in the Broadway theatre as a maker and user of new and old theatrical forms.

Odets, on the other hand, while describing himself as "a man of the Left," was, with the possible exception of his first play, *Waiting for Lefty*, no innovator where form was concerned. He attempted a poetic realism but it was still trying to represent real people in actual social relationships. And this was perhaps inevitable given his actor's temperament as well as his Marxist commitment; he had the revolutionary's eye on the great public, on the reconstitution of power once a failed capitalism had been brought down—for such was the Marxist and non-Marxist Left position on the proper moral obligation of the artist. But by temperament he was a poet seeking words that would lift him into a takeoff, regardless of his realist political commitments. O'Neill, on the other hand, was not the revolutionary but the rebel with a despairing anarchism in his heart. If he glimpsed any salvation, it was not to arrive in a more benign reconstitution of political power but in the tragic cleansing of the life-lie permanently ensconced in the human condition. Since he took no responsibility in theory for a new and better policy to take the place of the corrupted present one, he was free to explore all sorts of theatrical means by which to set forth the situation of the damned. Moreover, if O'Neill wanted his plays to register, and he surely did, they need not be popular to justify his having written them, for he was hunting the sounding whale of ultimate meaning, and he expected to suffer for it; oppositely, a critical or box-office failure for Odets meant rejection of a very personal kind, a spit in the eye by an ungrateful, self-satisfied bourgeois society. A failed play for Odets was a denial of what he was owed, for he was chasing the public no differently from his bourgeois nonrevolutionary contemporaries. O'Neill could say, and he did, that he was not interested in relations between men, but between Man and God. For America, in his view, was damned and if there were a few individuals who behaved justly and well it was not because they belonged to a particular social class or held a generous or unselfish political viewpoint, but by virtue of a grace whose source is beyond definition.

II

The realism of Broadway—and the Strand and the Boulevard theatre of France—was detested by the would-be poetic dramatists of my generation, just as it had always been since it came into vogue in the nineteenth century. What did this realism really come down to? A play representing real rather than symbolic or metaphysical persons and situations, its main virtue verisimilitude, with no revolutionary implications for society or even a symbolic statement of some general truth. Quite simply, conventional realism was conventional because it implicitly supported the conventions of society, but it could just as easily do something quite different, or so it seemed to me. Nevertheless, we thought it the perfect style for an unchallenging, simpleminded linear middle-class conformist view of life. What I found confusing at the time, however, was that not so very long before, the name "realism" had been applied to the revolutionary style of playwrights like Ibsen, Chekhov, and quite frequently Strindberg, writers whose whole thrust was in opposition to the bourgeois status quo and the hypocrisies on which it stood, or, in Chekhov's case, the futilities of the Czarist system.

My own first playwriting attempt was purely mimetic, a realistic play about my own family. It won me some prizes and productions, but, interestingly, I turned at once to a stylized treatment of life in a gigantic prison, modeled on Jackson State Penitentiary in Michigan —near Ann Arbor, where I was in school—the largest prison in the United States, which I had visited over weekends with a friend who was its lone psychologist. The theme of that play was that prisons existed to make desperate workingmen insane. There was a chorus of sane prisoners chanting from a high overpass above the stage, and a counter-chorus of the insane trying to draw the other into their ranks. It was inevitable that I had to confront the problem of dramatic language, for it was impossible to engage so vast a human disaster with speech born in a warm kitchen. I gradually came to wonder if the essential pressure toward poetic dramatic language—if not of stylization itself—came from the inclusion of society as a major element in the play's story or vision. Manifestly, prose realism was the language of the individual and of private life, poetry the language of man in crowds, in society. Put another way, prose is the language of family relations; it is the inclusion of the larger world beyond that naturally opens a play to the poetic.

But I wanted to succeed, I wanted to emerge and grip an audience. Minds might be illuminated by speeches thrown at them but it was by being moved that one was changed. And so the problem was that our audiences were trained, as it were, in a pawky realism and were turned off by stylistic novelty, by "art." How to find a style that would at one and the same time deeply engage an American audience, which insisted on a recognizable reality of characters, locales, and themes, while opening the stage to considerations of public morality and the mythic social fates—in short, the invisible?

Of course this was not my preoccupation alone. I doubt there was ever a time when there was so much discussion about form and style. T. S. Eliot was writing his verse plays, and Auden and Isherwood theirs; the poetic mimesis of Sean O'Casey was most popular; and W. B. Yeats's dialogue was studied if not very often produced. The impulse to poetry reached into the ex-newspaperman and realistic writer Maxwell Anderson, whose attempts to imitate Elizabethan prosody with contemporary characters and social themes were widely celebrated, as curios by some, as moving experiences by others.

To be just to Odets, it was he who challenged the Broadway theatre's addiction to verisimilitude by his idiosyncratic dialogue. And he was surely the first American playwright to be celebrated—and more wildly and lavishly than any other before him—for his writing style. For younger writers such as myself, Odets for a couple of years was the trailblazer; he was bringing the suffering of the

Great Depression onto the Broadway stage and making audiences listen. If he had not solved the problem of a contemporary American style, he had dared to invent an often wildly stylized stage speech. But I suppose that since his characters lacked elegance or strangeness, were, in fact, the very exemplars of realistic theatre, Odets was called a realist—indeed, a kind of reporter of Jewish life in the Bronx. I may not have lived in the Bronx but the speech of Brooklyn Jews certainly bore no resemblance to that of Odets's characters.

CARP [in *Golden Boy*]: I'm superdisgusted with you! . . . A man hits his wife and it's the first step to fascism! Look in the papers! On every side the clouds of war! . . . Ask yourself a pertinent remark; could a boy make a living playing this instrument [a violin] in our competitive civilization today?

ROXY: I think I'll run across the street and pick up an eight-cylinder sandwich.

The audiences roared with delight at these inventions. It was as though Odets were trying to turn dialogue into jazz. And his devotees went to his plays especially to pick up his latest deliciously improbable remarks and repeat them to their friends. Had any Bronxite—or anyone else in the century—really exclaimed, "God's teeth, no!" "What exhaust pipe did he crawl out of?" Lorna: "I feel like I'm shot from a cannon."

Inevitably, in a theatre bounded by realism, this had to be mistakenly labeled as accurate reportage, news from the netherworld. But of course it was an invented diction of a kind never heard before on stage—or off, for that matter. Odets's fervent ambition was to burst the bounds of Broadway while remaining inside its embrace, and if as time went on his lines began to seem self-consciously labored, no longer springing from characters but manifestly from the author and his will-to-poeticize, he at a minimum had made language the identifying mark of a playwright in America, and that was something that hadn't happened before.

Admittedly, I did not look at his style with objectivity but for its potential usefulness in breaking through the constricted realism of our theatre then. Odets was tremendously exciting to young writers. I was troubled by a tendency in his plays toward overtheatricalized excess, however—lines sometimes brought laughter where there should have been outrage, or pity, or some deeper emotion than amusement—and at times the plots verged on the schematic. Odets often overrhapsodized at the climaxes when he should have been reaching back to ancillary material that was not there. He wrote terrific scenes, blazing speeches and confrontations which showed what theatre could be, but with the exception, perhaps, of *Awake and Sing* and the racy *Golden Boy* he never wrote a play that lifted inexorably to its climactic revelation.

I came out of the thirties unsure whether there could be a viable counterform to the realism around me. All I knew for sure was that a good play must move forward in its depths as rapidly as on its surfaces; word-poetry wasn't enough if there was a fractured poetry in the structure, the gradually revealed illuminating idea behind the whole thing. A real play was the discovery of the unity of its contradictions; the essential poetry was the synthesis of even the least of its parts to form a symbolic meaning. Of course the problem had much to do with language but more primary was how to penetrate my own feelings about myself and the time in which I lived. Ideally, a good play must show as sound an emotional proof of its thesis as a case at law shows factual proof, and you can't do that with words alone, lovely as they might be.

Odets's contribution, ironically, was not his realistic portrayal of society—his alleged aim—but his willingness to be artificial; he brought back artificiality, if you will, just as ten years later Tennessee Williams did with his birdsong from the magnolias. But Williams had an advantage—his language could be far more faithful to its sources in reality. Southern people did love to talk, and in the accents Williams captured (as in *The Glass Menagerie*):

AMANDA: . . . But Laura is, thank heavens, not only pretty but also very domestic. I'm not at all. I never was a bit. I never could make a thing but angel-food cake. Well, in the South we had so many servants. Gone, gone, gone. All vestige of gracious living! Gone completely! I wasn't prepared for what the future brought me. All my gentlemen callers were sons of planters and so of course I assumed that I would be married to one and raise my family on a large piece of land with plenty of servants. But man proposes—and woman accepts the proposal!—To vary that old,

old saying a little bit—I married no planter! I married a man who worked for the telephone company! —That gallantly smiling gentleman over there! *(Points to husband's picture.)* A telephone man who—fell in love with long distance! Now he travels and I don't even know where! . . .

This too was called realism, and it probably was in the sense that there were people who talked like this. But then how did it differ from the conventional realistic play? Clearly, it was that the very action of Williams's plays, certainly the best of them, was working toward the building of symbolic meaning that would embrace both the psychological development of his characters and his personal specter of a menacing America struggling with its own sexuality and the anomie born of its dire materialism. In a word, Williams's style arose from his pain and anxiety at being overwhelmed and defeated by a gross violence that underlay the American—one might say the whole Western—ethos.

Their obsession with words notwithstanding, it was their need to communicate their resistance to something death-dealing in the culture that finally pressed Odets and Williams to address the big public and made them playwrights rather than sequestered poets. Stylistic invention without an implicit commitment of some kind to a more humane vision of life is a boat without rudder or cargo or destination—or worse, it is the occupation of the dilettante. Odets, when he began, thought his egalitarian Marxism would heal America and create its new community, but that ideology devolved into a rote religion before the thirties had even passed. Williams unfurled the banner of a forlorn but resisting heroism to the violence against the oddball, the poet, the sexual dissident. But it may as well be admitted that in their different ways both men in the end unwittingly collaborated with the monster they saw as trying to destroy them.

The plays these men wrote were shields raised against the many-arrowed darkness, but in the end there was little from outside to give them the spiritual support to complete their creative lives. Odets's best work ended with his rejection by Broadway and his move to Hollywood; Williams, likewise rejected, kept nevertheless to his trade, experimenting with forms and new methods that drew no encouragement from reviewers unable or unwilling to notice that the theatre culture had boxed in a writer of greatness who was struggling to find an audience in the passing crowd of a generation other than his own. At his strongest he had spoken for and to the center of society, in a style it could relate to, an enhanced, visionary realism. In the end a writer has no one to blame for his failings, not even himself, but the brutally dismissive glee of critics toward Williams's last plays simply laid more sticks on his burden. Toward the end he was still outside, scratching on the glass, as he had once put it, and it was the shadowed edges of life that drew him, the borderland where how things are said is everything, and everything has been said before.

The advent of the Absurd and of Beckett and his followers both obscured and illuminated the traditional elements of the discussion of theatre style. For O'Neill a good style was basically a question of the apt use of metaphor and argot. "God, if I could write like that!" he wrote to O'Casey, who, incidentally, would no doubt have labeled himself a realistic writer in the sense that he was giving his audiences the substance of their life conflicts. But like Williams, O'Casey came from a culture which loved talk and sucked on language like a sweet candy.

MRS. GROGAN: Oh, you've got a cold on you, Fluther.

FLUTHER: Oh, it's only a little one.

MRS. GROGAN: You'd want to be careful, all th' same. I knew a woman, a big lump of a woman, red-faced and round-bodied, a little awkward on her feet; you'd think, to look at her, she could put out her two arms an' lift a two-storied house on th' top of her head; got a ticklin' in her throat, an' a little cough, an' th' next mornin' she had a little catchin' in her chest, an' they had just time to wet her lips with a little rum, an' off she went.

(Juno and the Paycock)

Even in the most mundane of conversational exchanges O'Casey sought, and as often as not found, the lift of poetry. Indeed, that was the whole point—that the significantly poetic sprang from the raw and real experience of ordinary people. J. M. Synge, O'Casey's forerunner at the turn of the century, had struck a similar chord; Synge was in a supremely conscious revolt against the banality of most theatre language. As John Gassner noted, in Ireland the popular imagination was still, according to Synge, "fiery and magnificent, and tender; so that those of us who wish to write start with a chance that is not given to writers in places where the springtime of local life has been forgotten, and the harvest is a memory only, and the straw has been turned into bricks."

Synge rejected the then-dominant Ibsen and Zola for the "joyless and pallid words" of their realism and as in *Riders to the Sea*, when the women are lamenting the deaths of so many of their men working the angry sea:

MAURYA: In the big world the old people do be leaving things after them for their sons and children, but in this place it is the young men do be leaving things behind for them that do be old.

As far as style is concerned, the Beckett difference, as it might be called, was to introduce humble people—bums, in fact, or social sufferers—with the plainest of language, but arranged so as to announce and develop pure theme. His could be called a presentational thematic play, announcing what it was about and never straying very far from what it was conceived of to prove, or what his instinct had led him to confirm. Beckett had parted with inferential playwriting, where speeches inferred the author's thematic intentions while hewing to an apparently autonomous story building to a revelatory climax that united story and theme. In Beckett the story *was* the theme, inseparably so. Moreover, as will be shown in a moment, he interpreted the theme himself in his dialogue.

If—instead of the prewar poetic drama's requirement of an elevated tone or diction—the most common speech was now prized, it was not the speech of realistic plays. It was a speech skewed almost out of recognition by a surreal commitment to what at first had seemed to be the impotence of human hopes, and hence the futility of action itself. All but the flimsiest connections between speeches were eliminated, creating an atmosphere of sinister danger (in Pinter) or immanence (in Beckett). It was quite as though the emphatic absence of purpose in the characters had created a loss of syntax. It seems that in later years Beckett took pains to clarify this

impression of human futility, emphasizing the struggle *against* iner-
tia as his theme. In any case, however ridiculous so much of his
dialogue exchanges are, the tenderness of feeling in his work is
emphatically not that of the cynic or the hard ironist.

The dominating theme of *Godot* is stasis and the struggle to over-
come humanity's endlessly repetitious paralysis before the need to
act and change. We hear it plainly and stripped clean of plot or even
incident.

ESTRAGON: Then adieu.

POZZO: Adieu.

VLADIMIR: Adieu.

POZZO: Adieu.

Silence. No one moves.

VLADIMIR: Adieu.

POZZO: Adieu.

ESTRAGON: Adieu.

Silence.

POZZO: And thank you.

VLADIMIR: Thank *you.*

POZZO: Not at all.

ESTRAGON: Yes yes.

POZZO: No no.

VLADIMIR: Yes yes.

ESTRAGON: No no.

Silence.

POZZO: I don't seem to be able . . . *(long hesitation)* . . . to depart.

ESTRAGON: Such is life.

This is a vaudeville at the edge of the cliff, but vaudeville anyway, so I may be forgiven for being reminded of Jimmy Durante's ditty— "Didja ever get the feelin' that you wanted to go? But still you had the feelin' that you wanted to stay?"

It is a language shorn of metaphor, simile, everything but its instructions, so to speak. The listener hears the theme like a nail drawn across a pane of glass.

So the struggle with what might be called reportorial realism, written "the way people talk," is at least as old as the century. As for myself, my own tendency has been to shift styles according to the nature of my subject. *All My Sons, The Crucible, A View from the Bridge, Death of a Salesman, The Price, The American Clock,* my earliest work, like *The Golden Years,* about the destruction of Mexico by the Spaniards, and the more recent plays, like *The Creation of the World, Some Kind of Love Story,* and *The Last Yankee,* differ very much in their language. This, in order to find speech that springs naturally out of the characters and their backgrounds rather than imposing a general style. If my approach to playwriting is partly literary, I hope it is well hidden. Leroy Hamilton is a native New England carpenter and speaks like one, and not like the New York working men and women in *A Memory of Two Mondays,* or Eddie Carbone, who comes out of a quite different culture.

So the embrace of something called realism is obviously very wide; it can span the distance between a Turgenev and a Becque, between Wedekind and your latest Broadway hit. The main thing I sought in *The Last Yankee* was to make real my sense of the life of such people, the kind of man swinging the hammer through a lifetime, the kind of woman waiting forever for her ship to come in. And second, my view of their present confusion and, if you will, decay and possible recovery. They are bedrock, aspiring not to greatness but to other gratifications—successful parenthood, decent children and a decent house and a decent car and an occasional nice evening with family or friends, and above all, of course, some financial security. Needless to say, they are people who can be inspired to great and noble sacrifice, but also to bitter hatreds. As the world goes I suppose they are the luckiest people, but some of them—a great many, in fact—have grown ill with what would once have been called a sickness of the soul.

And that is the subject of the play, its "matter." For depression is far from being merely a question of an individual's illness, although it appears as that, of course; it is at the same time, most especially in Patricia Hamilton's case, the grip on her of a success mythology which is both naïve and brutal, and which, to her misfortune, she has made her own. And opposing it, quite simply, is her husband Leroy's incredibly enduring love for her, for nature and the world.

A conventionally realistic play would no doubt have attempted to create a "just-like-life" effect, with the sickness gradually rising out of the normal routines of the family's life, and calling up our empathy by virtue of our instant identification with familiar reality. But while Patricia Hamilton, the carpenter's wife, is seen as an individual sufferer, the context of her illness is equally important because, for one thing, she knows, as do many such patients, that more Americans (and West Europeans) are in hospitals for depression than for any other ailment. In life, with such people, a high degree of objectification or distancing exists, and the style of the play had to reflect the fact that they commonly know a great deal about the social setting of the illness even as they are unable to tear themselves free of it. And this affects the play's style.

It opens by directly, even crudely, grasping the core of its central preoccupation—the moral and social myths feeding the disease; and we have a discussion of the hospital's enormous parking lot, a conversation bordering on the absurd. I would call this realism, but it is far from the tape-recorded kind. Frick, like Leroy Hamilton, has arrived for a visit with his wife, and after a moment's silence while the two strangers grope for a conversational opening . . .

FRICK: Tremendous parking space down there. 'They need that for?

LEROY: Well a lot of people visit on weekends. Fills up pretty much.

FRICK: Really? That whole area?

LEROY: Pretty much.

FRICK: 'Doubt that.

The play is made of such direct blows aimed at the thematic center; there is a vast parking space because crowds of stricken citizens converge on this place to visit mothers, fathers, brothers, and sisters. So that the two patients we may be about to meet are not at all unique. This is in accord with the vision of the play, which is intended to be both close up and wide, psychological and social, subjective and objective, and manifestly so. To be sure, there is a realistic tone to this exchange—people do indeed seem to talk this way—but an inch below is the thematic selectivity which drives the whole tale. Perhaps it needs to be said that this split vision has informed all the plays I have written. I have tried to make things seen in their social context and simultaneously felt as intimate testimony, and that requires a style, but one that draws as little attention to itself as possible, for I would wish a play to be absorbed rather than merely observed.

I have called this play a comedy, a comedy about a tragedy, and I am frankly not sure why. Possibly it is due to the absurdity of people constantly comparing themselves to others—something we all do to one degree or another, but in Patricia's case to the point of illness.

PATRICIA: There was something else you said. About standing on line.

LEROY: On line?

PATRICIA: That you'll always be at the head of the line because . . . *breaks off.*

LEROY: I'm the only one on it. . . . We're really all on a one-person line, Pat. I learned that in these years.

The play's language, then, has a surface of everyday realism, but its action is overtly stylized rather than "natural."

Finally, a conventionally realistic work about mental illness would be bound to drive to a reverberating climax. But repression is the cultural inheritance of these New Englanders and such theatricality would be a betrayal of *their* style of living and dying. Indeed, short of suicide, the illness, properly speaking, never ends in the sense of tying all the loose strings, nor should the play, which simply sets the boundaries of the possible. For the theme is hope rather than completion or achievement, and hope is tentative always.

A play about them should have a certain amplitude of sound, nothing greater or less, reflecting their tight yet often deeply felt culture. And in a play about them they should recognize themselves —and even possibly what drives them mad—just like the longshoremen who saw themselves in *A View from the Bridge* or the cops in *The Price* or the salespeople in *Death of a Salesman.* That would be a satisfactory realism as I saw it.

I suppose the form itself of *The Last Yankee* is as astringently direct and uncluttered as it is because these people are supremely the prey of the culture, if only because it is never far from the center of their minds—the latest film or TV show, the economy's ups and downs, and above all the endless advertising-encouraged self-comparisons with others who are more or less successful than they. This ritualistic preoccupation is at the play's dramatic core and, I felt, ought not be unclear or misted over, for it is from its grip they must be freed if they are ever to be free at all. Hence, the repeated references to ambition, to success and failure, to wealth and poverty, to economic survival, to the kind of car one drives and the suit one wears. In a word, the play could not be amorphously "realistic" if it was to reflect the obsessiveness of the characters in life. So if *The Last Yankee* is realism it is of this kind resulting from an intense selectivity, which in turn is derived from the way these people live and feel.

But obviously, to make such a strictly thematic play demands intense condensation and the syncopating of idea and feeling and language. More than one actor in my plays has told me that it is surprisingly difficult to memorize the dialogue. It sounds like real, almost like reported talk, when in fact it is intensely composed, compressed, "angled" into an inevitability that seems natural but isn't. For it is always necessary to employ the artificial in order to arrive at the real. So that the question I bring to a play is not whether its form and style are new or old, experimental or traditional, but first, whether it brings news, something truly felt by its author, something thought through to its conclusion and its significance; and second, whether its form is beautiful, or wasteful, whether it is aberrant for aberrancy's sake, full of surprises that discover little, and so on.

Something called Realism can land us further from common reality than the most fantastic caprice. But in the end, if stylization in theatre needs justification—and it does, of course—it is not in its novelty but in its enhancement of discovery of how life works in our time. How a thing is said is therefore only as important as what it is saying. The proof is the deep pile of experimental plays of two, three, five, ten years ago, which can be appreciated now only by the scholar-specialist, a pile, incidentally, no smaller than the one for so many realistic plays of the same era. So finding the truth is no easier now when we are totally free to use any stylistic means at hand than it was a century or half a century ago when a play had to be "real" to even be read, and had to make sense to sensible people.

Call it a question of personal taste rather than principle, but I think that in theatre work there is an optimum balance between two kinds of approaches. One is the traditional attempt to fill characters with acknowledged emotion, "as in life." The other is, in effect, to evacuate emotion from characters and merely refer to it rather than acting it out. Brecht, for one, tried to do this and failed, excepting in his most agitprop and forgettable plays. Actually, the strict containment not of emotion but of emotionalism is the hallmark of the Greek tragic plays, of Molière and Racine and the Japanese No plays, while Shakespeare, it seems to me, is the balance, the fusion of idea and feeling. In short, it is by no means the abstracting of emotion I dislike; on the contrary, it is the lack of it and the substitution for it of fashionably alienated ironies.

As I am not a critic and would not do anything to make any writer's life harder, I will desist from naming names, but there has been a plethora of plays in recent years whose claim to modernity is based on indicated rather than felt emotion, on the assumption, I suppose, that this *sec* quality intellectualizes a work and saves it from the banality associated with writing aimed at the audience's belly rather than at its head. The devil to be avoided is, of course, sentimentality—emotion unearned. But emotion can be earned, of course. Yet a play that is not camp and moves people is in danger of dismissal. (Unless it appears in old films, which we allow ourselves to be moved by if at the same instant we can protect our modernity by feeling superior to their time-bound naïveté.) But if the pun can be pardoned, man lives not by head alone, and the balance between the two modes, one aimed at the mind and one at the flesh, as it were, is what will interpret life more fully, rather than headline it with conceptualizations that too often simply clump about on the stilts of dry irony that time and the shifts of cultural politics will make thoroughly disposable. After all, at least part of the aim of a modern play must be to show what life now *feels like*.

Ultimately every assault on the human mystery falls back to the ground, changing little, but the flight of the arrow continues claiming our attention over more time when its direction is toward the castle rather than the wayward air.

Broken Glass

CAST OF CHARACTERS

Phillip Gellburg

Sylvia Gellburg

Dr. Harry Hyman

Margaret Hyman

Harriet

Stanton Case

*The play takes place in Brooklyn in the last days
of November 1938.*

SCENE ONE

A lone cellist is discovered, playing a simple tune. The tune finishes. Light goes out on the cellist and rises on . . .

Office of Dr. Harry Hyman in his home. Alone on stage Phillip Gellburg, a slender, intense man in his late forties, waits in perfect stillness, legs crossed. He is in a black suit, black tie and shoes and white shirt. Margaret Hyman, the doctor's wife, enters. She is fair, lusty, energetic, carrying pruning shears.

MARGARET: He'll be right with you, he's just changing. Can I get you something? Tea?

GELLBURG, *faint reprimand:* He said five o'clock sharp.

MARGARET: He was held up in the hospital, that new union's pulled a strike, imagine? A strike in a hospital? It's incredible. And his horse went lame.

GELLBURG: His horse?

MARGARET: He rides on Ocean Parkway every afternoon.

GELLBURG, *attempting easy familiarity:* Oh yes, I heard about that . . . it's very nice. You're Mrs. Hyman?

MARGARET: I've nodded to you on the street for years now, but you're too preoccupied to notice.

GELLBURG, *a barely hidden boast:* Lot on my mind, usually. *A certain amused loftiness.* —So you're his nurse, too.

MARGARET: We met in Mount Sinai when he was interning. He's lived to regret it. *She laughs in a burst.*

GELLBURG: That's some laugh you've got there. I sometimes hear you all the way down the block to my house.

MARGARET: Can't help it, my whole family does it. I'm originally from Minnesota. It's nice to meet you finally, Mr. Goldberg.

GELLBURG: It's Gellburg, not Goldberg.

MARGARET: Oh, I'm sorry.

GELLBURG: G-e-l-l-b-u-r-g. It's the only one in the phone book.

MARGARET: It does sound like Goldberg.

GELLBURG: But it's not, it's Gellburg. *A distinction.* We're from Finland originally.

MARGARET: Oh! We came from Lithuania . . . Kazauskis?

GELLBURG, *put down momentarily:* Don't say.

MARGARET, *trying to charm him to his ease:* Ever been to Minnesota?

GELLBURG: New York State's the size of France, what would I go to Minnesota for?

MARGARET: Nothing. Just there's a lot of Finns there.

GELLBURG: Well, there's Finns all over.

MARGARET, *defeated, shows the clipper:* . . . I'll get back to my roses. Whatever it is I hope you'll be feeling better.

GELLBURG: It's not me.

MARGARET: Oh. Cause you seem a little pale.

GELLBURG: Me? —I'm always this color. It's my wife.

MARGARET: I'm sorry to hear that, she's a lovely woman. It's nothing serious, is it?

GELLBURG: He's just had a specialist put her through some tests, I'm waiting to hear. I think it's got him mystified.

MARGARET: Well, I mustn't butt in. *Makes to leave but can't resist.* Can you say what it is?

GELLBURG: She can't walk.

MARGARET: What do you mean?

GELLBURG, *an overtone of protest of some personal victimization:* Can't stand up. No feeling in her legs. —I'm sure it'll pass, but it's terrible.

MARGARET: But I only saw her in the grocery . . . can't be more than ten days ago . . .

GELLBURG: It's nine days today.

MARGARET: But she's such a wonderful looking woman. Does she have fever?

GELLBURG: No.

MARGARET: Thank God, then it's not Polio.

GELLBURG: No, she's in perfect health otherwise.

MARGARET: Well Harry'll get to the bottom of it if anybody can. They call him from everywhere for opinions, you know . . . Boston,

Chicago . . . By rights he ought to be on Park Avenue if he only had the ambition, but he always wanted a neighborhood practice. Why, I don't know—we never invite anybody, we never go out, all our friends are in Manhattan. But it's his nature, you can't fight a person's nature. Like me for instance, I like to talk and I like to laugh. You're not much of a talker, are you.

GELLBURG, *purse-mouthed smile:* When I can get a word in edgewise.

MARGARET, *burst of laughter:* Ha! —So you've got a sense of humor after all. Well, give my best to Mrs. Goldberg.

GELLBURG: Gellbu . . .

MARGARET, *hits her own head:* Gellburg, excuse me! —It practically sounds like Goldberg . . .

GELLBURG: No-no, look in the phonebook, it's the only one, G-e-l-l . . .

Enter Dr. Hyman.

MARGARET, *with a little wave to Gellburg:* Be seeing you!

GELLBURG: Be in good health.

Margaret exits.

HYMAN, *in his early fifties, a conventionally handsome man, but underneath a determined scientific idealist. Settling behind his desk chuckling:* She chew your ear off?

GELLBURG, *his worldly mode:* Not too bad, I've had worse.

HYMAN: Well, there's no way around it, women are talkers . . . *Grinning familiarly.* But try living without them, right?

GELLBURG: Without women?

HYMAN, *he sees Gellburg has flushed; there is a short hiatus, then . . . :* Well, never mind. —I'm glad you could make it tonight, I wanted to talk to you before I see your wife again tomorrow. Smoke?

GELLBURG: No thanks, never have. Isn't it bad for you?

HYMAN: Certainly is. *Lights a cigar.* But more people die of rat bite, you know.

GELLBURG: Rat bite!

HYMAN: Oh yes, but they're mostly the poor so it's not an interesting statistic. Have you seen her tonight or did you come here from the office?

GELLBURG: I thought I'd see you before I went home. But I phoned her this afternoon—same thing, no change.

HYMAN: How's she doing with the wheelchair?

GELLBURG: Better, she can get herself in and out of the bed now.

HYMAN: Good. And she manages the bathroom?

GELLBURG: Oh yes. I got the maid to come in the mornings to help her take a bath, clean up . . .

HYMAN: Good. Your wife has a lot of courage, I admire that kind of woman. My wife is similar; I like the type.

GELLBURG: What type you mean?

HYMAN: You know—vigorous. I mean mentally and . . . you know, just generally. Moxie.

GELLBURG: Oh.

HYMAN: Forget it, it was only a remark.

GELLBURG: No, you're right, I never thought of it, but she is unusually that way.

HYMAN, *pause. Some prickliness here which he can't understand:* Doctor Sherman's report . . .

GELLBURG: What's he say?

HYMAN: I'm getting to it.

GELLBURG: Oh. Beg your pardon.

HYMAN: You'll have to bear with me . . . may I call you Phillip?

GELLBURG: Certainly.

HYMAN: I don't express my thoughts very quickly, Phillip.

GELLBURG: Likewise. Go ahead, take your time.

HYMAN: People tend to overestimate the wisdom of physicians so I try to think things through before I speak to a patient.

GELLBURG: I'm glad to hear that.

HYMAN: Aesculapius stuttered, you know—ancient Greek god of medicine. But probably based on a real physician who hesitated about giving advice. Somerset Maugham stammered, studied medicine. Anton Chekhov, great writer, also a doctor had tuberculosis. Doctors are very often physically defective in some way, that's why they're interested in healing. *A certain pretentiousness.* —This is all psychology.

GELLBURG, *impressed:* I see.

HYMAN: I'll tell you why I'm saying all this; it's that we are in the realm of psychology with your wife, Phillip.

GELLBURG: I'm glad to hear you say that. —I've been thinking the same thing—I think this was brought on by some kind of scare.

HYMAN: Well that's interesting, let's talk about that in a minute. *Pause —Thinks.* I find this Adolf Hitler very disturbing. You been following him in the papers?

GELLBURG: Well yes, but not much. My average day in the office is ten, eleven hours.

HYMAN: They've been smashing the Jewish stores in Berlin all week, you know.

GELLBURG: Oh yes, I saw that again yesterday.

HYMAN: Very disturbing. Forcing old men to scrub the sidewalks with toothbrushes. On the Kurfürstendamm, that's equivalent to Fifth Avenue. Nothing but hoodlums in uniform.

GELLBURG: My wife is very upset about that.

HYMAN: I know, that's why I mention it. *Hesitates.* And how about you?

GELLBURG: Of course. It's a terrible thing. Why do you ask?

HYMAN, *a smile:* —I don't know, I got the feeling she may be afraid she's annoying you when she talks about such things.

GELLBURG: Why? I don't mind. —She said she's annoying me?

HYMAN: Not in so many words, but . . .

GELLBURG: I can't believe she'd say a thing like . . .

HYMAN: Wait a minute, I didn't say she said it . . .

GELLBURG: She doesn't annoy me but what can be done about such things? The thing is, she doesn't like to hear about the other side of it.

HYMAN: What other side?

GELLBURG: It's no excuse for what's happening over there but German Jews can be pretty . . . you know . . . *Pushes up his nose with his forefinger.* Not that they're pushy like the ones from Poland or Russia but friend of mine's in the garment industry; these German Jews won't take an ordinary good job, you know; it's got to be pretty high up in the firm or they're insulted. And they can't even speak English.

HYMAN: Well I guess a lot of them were pretty important over there.

GELLBURG: I know, but they're supposed to be *refugees,* aren't they? With all our unemployment you'd think they'd appreciate a little more. Latest official figure is twelve million unemployed you know, and it's probably bigger but Roosevelt can't admit it, after the fortune he's pouring into WPA and the rest of that welfare *mishugas.* —But she's not *annoying* me, for God's sake.

HYMAN: . . . I just thought I'd mention it; but it was only a feeling I had . . .

GELLBURG: I'll tell you right now, I don't run with the crowd, I see with these eyes, nobody else's.

HYMAN: I see that. —You're very unusual—*Grinning.* —You almost sound like a Republican.

GELLBURG: Why? —The Torah says a Jew has to be a Democrat? I didn't get where I am by agreeing with everybody.

HYMAN: Well that's a good thing; you're independent. *Nods, puffs.* You know, what mystifies me is that the Germans I knew in Heidelberg . . . I took my MD there . . .

GELLBURG: You got along with them.

HYMAN: Some of the finest people I ever met.

GELLBURG: Well, there you go.

HYMAN: We had a marvelous student choral group, fantastic voices; Saturday nights, we'd have a few beers and go singing through the streets. . . . People'd applaud from the windows.

GELLBURG: Don't say.

HYMAN: I simply can't imagine those people marching into Austria, and now they say Czechoslovakia's next, and Poland . . . But fanatics have taken Germany, I guess, and they can be brutal, you know . . .

GELLBURG: Listen, I sympathize with these refugees, but . . .

HYMAN, *cutting him off:* I had quite a long talk with Sylvia yesterday, I suppose she told you?

GELLBURG, *a tensing:* Well . . . no, she didn't mention. What about?

HYMAN, *surprised by Sylvia's omission:* . . . Well, about her condition, and . . . just in passing . . . your relationship.

GELLBURG: *My* relationship?

HYMAN: . . . It was just in passing.

GELLBURG: Why, what'd she say?

HYMAN: Well, that you . . . get along very well.

GELLBURG: Oh.

HYMAN, *encouragingly, as he sees Gellburg's small tension:* I found her a remarkably well-informed woman. Especially for this neighborhood.

GELLBURG, *a pridefully approving nod; relieved that he can speak of her positively:* That's practically why we got together in the first place. I don't exaggerate, if Sylvia was a man she could have run the Federal Reserve. You could talk to Sylvia like you talk to a man.

HYMAN: I'll bet.

GELLBURG, *his purse-mouthed grin:* . . . Not that talking was all we did—but you turn your back on Sylvia and she's got her nose in a book or a magazine. I mean there's not one woman in ten around here could even tell you who their Congressman is. And you can throw in the men, too. *Pause.* So where are we?

HYMAN: Doctor Sherman confirms my diagnosis. I ask you to listen carefully, will you?

GELLBURG, *brought up:* Of course, that's why I came.

HYMAN: We can find no physical reason for her inability to walk.

GELLBURG: No physical reason . . .

HYMAN: We are almost certain that this is a psychological condition.

GELLBURG: But she's numb, she has no feeling in her legs.

HYMAN: Yes. This is what we call an hysterical paralysis. Hysterical doesn't mean she screams and yells . . .

GELLBURG: Oh, I know. It means like . . . ah . . . *Bumbles off.*

HYMAN, *a flash of umbrage, dislike:* Let me explain what it means, okay? —Hysteria comes from the Greek word for the womb because it was thought to be a symptom of female anxiety. Of course it isn't, but that's where it comes from. People who are anxious enough or really frightened can imagine they've gone blind or deaf, for instance . . . and they really can't see or hear. It was sometimes called shell-shock during the War.

GELLBURG: You mean . . . you don't mean she's . . . crazy.

HYMAN: We'll have to talk turkey, Phillip. If I'm going to do you any good. I'm going to have to ask you some personal questions. Some of them may sound raw, but I've only been superficially acquainted with Sylvia's family and I need to know more . . .

GELLBURG: She says you treated her father . . .

HYMAN: Briefly; a few visits shortly before he passed away. They're fine people. I hate like Hell to see this happen to her, you see what I mean?

GELLBURG: You can tell it to me; is she crazy?

HYMAN: Phillip, are you? Am I? In one way or another who isn't crazy? The main difference is that our kind of crazy still allows us to walk around and tend to our business. But who knows? —People like us may be the craziest of all.

GELLBURG, *scoffing grin:* Why!

HYMAN: Because we don't know we're nuts and the other kind does.

GELLBURG: I don't know about that . . .

HYMAN: Well, it's neither here nor there.

GELLBURG: I certainly don't think *I'm* nuts.

HYMAN: I wasn't saying that . . .

GELLBURG: What do you mean, then?

HYMAN, *grinning:* You're not an easy man to talk to, are you.

GELLBURG: Why? If I don't understand I have to ask, don't I?

HYMAN: Yes, you're right.

GELLBURG: That's the way I am—they don't pay me for being easy to talk to.

HYMAN: You're in . . . real estate?

GELLBURG: I'm head of the Mortgage Department of Brooklyn Guarantee and Trust.

HYMAN: Oh, that's right, she told me.

GELLBURG: We are the largest lender east of the Mississippi.

HYMAN: Really. *Fighting deflation.* Well, let me tell you my approach; if possible I'd like to keep her out of that whole psychiatry rigmarole. Not that I'm against it, but I think you get further faster, sometimes, with a little common sense and some plain human sympathy. Can we talk turkey? *Tuchas offen tisch,* you know any Yiddish?

GELLBURG: Yes, it means get your ass on the table.

HYMAN: Correct. So let's forget crazy and try to face the facts. We have a strong, healthy woman who has no physical ailment, and suddenly can't stand on her legs. Why?

He goes silent. Gellburg shifts uneasily.

I don't mean to embarrass you . . .

GELLBURG, *an angry smile:* You're not embarrassing me. —What do you want to know?

HYMAN, *sets himself, then launches:* In these cases there is often a sexual disability. You have relations, I imagine?

GELLBURG: Relations? Yes, we have relations.

HYMAN, *a softening smile:* Often?

GELLBURG: What's that got to do with it?

HYMAN: Sex could be connected. You don't have to answer . . .

GELLBURG: No-no it's all right . . . I would say it depends—maybe twice, three times a week.

HYMAN, *seems surprised:* Well that's good. She seems satisfied?

GELLBURG, *shrugs; hostilely:* I guess she is, sure.

HYMAN: That was a foolish question, forget it.

GELLBURG, *flushed:* Why, did she mention something about this?

HYMAN: Oh no, it's just something I thought of later.

GELLBURG: Well, I'm no Rudolph Valentino but I . . .

HYMAN: Rudolph Valentino probably wasn't either. —You mentioned she got scared.

GELLBURG, *relieved to be off the other subject:* If you ask me I think it was when they started putting all the pictures in the paper. About these Nazi carryings-on. I noticed she started . . . staring at them . . . in a very peculiar way. And . . . I don't know. It made her angry or something.

HYMAN: At you.

GELLBURG: Well . . . *Nods, agreeing* . . . in general. —Personally I don't think they should be publishing those kind of pictures.

HYMAN: Why not?

GELLBURG: She scares herself to death with them—three thousand miles away, and what does it accomplish! Except maybe put some fancy new ideas into these anti-Semites walking around New York here.

Slight pause.

HYMAN: Tell me how she collapsed. You were going to the movies . . . ?

GELLBURG, *breathing more deeply:* Yes. We were just starting down the porch steps and all of a sudden her . . . *Difficulty; he breaks off.*

HYMAN: I'm sorry but I . . .

GELLBURG: . . . Her legs turned to butter. I couldn't stand her up. Kept falling around like a rag doll. I had to carry her into the house. And she kept apologizing . . . ! *He weeps; recovers.* I can't talk about it.

HYMAN: It's all right.

GELLBURG: She's always been such a level-headed woman. *Weeping threatens again.* I don't know what to do. She's my life.

HYMAN: I'll do my best for her, Phillip, she's a wonderful woman. —Let's talk about something else. What do you do exactly?

GELLBURG: I mainly evaluate properties.

HYMAN: Whether to grant a mortgage . . .

GELLBURG: And how big a one and the terms.

HYMAN: How's the Depression hit you?

GELLBURG: Well, it's no comparison with '32 to '36, let's say—we were foreclosing left and right in those days. But we're on our feet and running.

HYMAN: And you head the department . . .

GELLBURG: Above me is only Mr. Case. Stanton Wylie Case; he's chairman and president. You're not interested in boat racing.

HYMAN: Why?

GELLBURG: His yacht won the America's cup two years ago. For the second time. The Aurora?

HYMAN: Oh yes! I think I read about . . .

GELLBURG: He's had me aboard twice.

HYMAN: Really.

GELLBURG, *the grin:* The only Jew ever set foot on that deck.

HYMAN: Don't say.

GELLBURG: In fact, I'm the only Jew ever worked for Brooklyn Guarantee in their whole history.

HYMAN: That so.

GELLBURG: Oh yes. And they go back to the 1890's. Started right out of accountancy school and moved straight up. They've been wonderful to me; it's a great firm.

A long moment as Hyman stares at Gellburg who is proudly positioned now, absorbing his poise from the evoked memories of his success. Gradually Gellburg turns to him.

How could this be a mental condition?

HYMAN: It's unconscious; like . . . well, take yourself; I notice you're all in black. Can I ask you why?

GELLBURG: I've worn black since high school.

HYMAN: No particular reason.

GELLBURG, *shrugs:* Always liked it, that's all.

HYMAN: Well, it's a similar thing with her; she doesn't know why she's doing this, but some very deep, hidden part of her mind is directing her to do it. You don't agree.

GELLBURG: I don't know.

HYMAN: You think she knows what she's doing?

GELLBURG: Well I always liked black for business reasons.

HYMAN: It gives you authority?

GELLBURG: Not exactly authority, but I wanted to look a little older. See, I graduated high school at fifteen and I was only twenty-two when I entered the firm. But I knew what I was doing.

HYMAN: Then you think she's doing this on purpose?

GELLBURG: —Except she's numb; nobody can purposely do that, can they?

HYMAN: I don't think so. —I tell you, Phillip, not really knowing your wife, if you have any idea why she could be doing a thing like this . . .

GELLBURG: I told you, I don't know.

HYMAN: Nothing occurs to you.

GELLBURG, *an edge of irritation:* I can't think of anything.

HYMAN: I'll tell you a funny thing, talking to her she doesn't seem all that unhappy.

GELLBURG: Say! —Yes, that's what I mean. That's exactly what I mean. It's like she's almost . . . I don't know . . . enjoying herself. I mean in a way.

HYMAN: How could that be possible?

GELLBURG: Of course she apologizes for it, and for making it hard for me—you know, like I have to do a lot of the cooking now, and tending to my laundry and so on . . . I even shop for groceries and the butcher . . . and change the sheets . . .

He breaks off with some realization. Hyman doesn't speak. A long pause.

You mean . . . she's doing it against me?

Stares for a long moment, then makes to rise, obviously deeply disturbed.

HYMAN: I don't know, what do *you* think?

GELLBURG: I'd better be getting home. *Lost in his own thought.* I don't know whether to ask you this or not.

HYMAN: What's to lose, go ahead.

GELLBURG: My parents were from the old country, you know, —I don't know if it was in Poland someplace or Russia—but there was this woman who they say was . . . you know . . . gotten into by a . . . like the ghost of a dead person . . .

HYMAN: A dybbuk.

GELLBURG: That's it. And it made her lose her mind and so forth. —You believe in that? They had to get a Rabbi to pray it out of her body. But you think that's possible?

HYMAN: Do I think so? No. Do you?

GELLBURG: Oh no. It just crossed my mind.

HYMAN: Well I wouldn't know how to pray it out of her, so . . .

GELLBURG: Be straight with me—is she going to come out of this?

HYMAN: Well, let's talk again after I see her tomorrow. Maybe I should tell you . . . I have this unconventional approach to illness, Phillip. Especially where the mental element is involved. I believe we get sick in two's and three's and four's, not alone as individuals. You follow me? I want you to do me a favor, will you?

GELLBURG: What's that.

HYMAN: You won't be offended, okay?

GELLBURG, *tensely:* Why should I be offended?

HYMAN: I'd like you to give her a lot of loving. *Fixing Gellburg in his gaze.* Can you? It's important now.

GELLBURG: Say, you're not blaming this on me, are you?

HYMAN: What's the good of blame? —From here on out *tuchas offen tisch,* okay? And Phillip?

GELLBURG: Yes?

HYMAN: Try not to let yourself get mad.

Gellburg turns and goes out. Hyman returns to his desk, makes some notes. Margaret enters.

MARGARET: That's one miserable little pisser.

Hyman writes, doesn't look up.

He's a dictator, you know. I was just remembering when I went to the grandmother's funeral? He stands outside the funeral parlor and decides who's going to sit with who in the limousines for the cemetery. "You sit with him, you sit with her . . ." And they obey him like he owned the funeral!

HYMAN: Did you find out what's playing?

MARGARET: At the Beverly they've got Ginger Rogers and Fred Astaire. Jimmy Cagney's at the Rialto but it's another gangster story.

HYMAN: I'm beginning to get a sour feeling about this thing; I barely know my way around psychiatry. I'm not completely sure I ought to get into it.

MARGARET: Why not? —She's a very beautiful woman.

HYMAN, *matching her wryness:* Well, is that a reason to turn her away? *He laughs, grasps her hand.* Something about it fascinates me—no disease and she's paralyzed. I'd really love to give it a try. I mean I don't want to turn myself into a post office, shipping all the hard cases to specialists, the woman's sick and I'd like to help.

MARGARET: But if you're not getting anywhere in a little while you'll promise to send her to somebody.

HYMAN: Absolutely. *Committed now: full enthusiasm.* I just feel there's something about it that I understand. —Let's see Cagney.

MARGARET: Oh no, Fred Astaire.

HYMAN: That's what I meant. Come here.

MARGARET, *as he embraces her:* We should leave now . . .

HYMAN: You're the best, Margaret.

MARGARET: A lot of good it does me.

HYMAN: If it really bothers you I'll get someone else to take the case.

MARGARET: You won't, you know you won't. *He is lifting her skirt.* Don't, Harry. Come on. *She frees her skirt, he kisses her breasts.*

HYMAN: Should I tell you what I'd like to do with you?

MARGARET: Tell me, yes, tell me. And make it wonderful.

HYMAN: We find an island and we strip and go riding on this white horse . . .

MARGARET: Together.

HYMAN: You in front.

MARGARET: Naturally.

HYMAN: And then we go swimming . . .

MARGARET: Harry, that's lovely.

HYMAN: And I hire this shark to swim very close and we just manage to get out of the water, and we're so grateful to be alive we fall down on the beach together and . . .

MARGARET, *pressing his lips shut:* Sometimes you're so good. *She kisses him.*

Blackout.

SCENE TWO

The lone cellist plays. then lights go down.

Next evening. The Gellburg house. Sylvia Gellburg is seated in a wheelchair reading a newspaper. Beside her, an upholstered chair. She is in mid-forties, a buxom, capable and warm woman. Right now her hair is brushed down to her shoulders, and she is in a nightgown and robe. She reads the paper with an intense, almost haunted interest, looking up now and then to visualize.

Her sister Harriet, a couple of years younger. Wears a dress and carries a pocketbook.

HARRIET: So what do you want, steak or chicken? Or maybe he'd like chops for a change.

SYLVIA: Please, don't put yourself out, Phillip doesn't mind a little shopping.

HARRIET: What's the matter with you, I'm going anyway, he's got enough on his mind.

SYLVIA: Well all right, get a couple of chops.

HARRIET: And what about you. You have to start eating!

SYLVIA: I'm eating.

HARRIET: What, a piece of cucumber? Look how pale you are. And what is this with newspapers night and day?

SYLVIA: I like to see what's happening.

HARRIET: I don't know about this doctor. Maybe you need a specialist.

SYLVIA: He brought one two days ago, Doctor Sherman. From Mount Sinai.

HARRIET: Really? And?

SYLVIA: We're waiting to hear. I like Doctor Hyman.

HARRIET: Nobody in the family ever had anything like this. You feel *something*, though, don't you?

SYLVIA, *pause. She lifts her face:* Yes . . . but inside, not on the skin. *Looks at her legs.* I can harden the muscles but I can't lift them. *Strokes her thighs.* I seem to have an ache. Not only here but . . . *She runs her hands down her trunk.* my whole body seems . . . I can't describe it. It's like I was just born and I . . . didn't want to come out yet. Like a deep, terrible aching . . .

HARRIET: Didn't want to come out yet! What are you talking about?

SYLVIA, *sighs gently, knowing Harriet can never understand:* Maybe if he has a nice duck. If not, get the chops. And thanks, Harriet, it's sweet of you. —By the way, what did David decide?

HARRIET: He's not going to college.

SYLVIA, *shocked:* I don't believe it! With a scholarship and he's not going?

HARRIET: What can we do? *Resignedly.* He says college wouldn't help him get a job anyway.

SYLVIA: Harriet, that's terrible! —Listen, tell him I have to talk to him.

HARRIET: Would you! I was going to ask you but with this happening *indicates her legs*. I didn't think you'd . . .

SYLVIA: Never mind, tell him to come over. And you must tell Murray he's got to put his foot down—you've got a brilliant boy! My God . . . *Picks up newspaper* . . . if I'd had a chance to go to college I'd have had a whole different life, you can't let this happen.

HARRIET: I'll tell David. . . . I wish I knew what is suddenly so interesting in a newspaper. This is not normal, Sylvia, is it?

SYLVIA, *pause. She stares ahead:* They are making old men crawl around and clean the sidewalks with toothbrushes.

HARRIET: Who is?

SYLVIA: In Germany. Old men with beards!

HARRIET: So why are you so interested in that? What business of yours is that?

SYLVIA, *slight pause; searches within:* I don't really know. *A slight pause.* Remember Grandpa? His eyeglasses with the bent side-piece? One of the old men in the paper was his spitting image, he had the same exact glasses with the wire frames. I can't get it out of my mind. On their knees on the sidewalk, two old men. And there's fifteen or twenty people standing in a circle laughing at them scrubbing with toothbrushes. There's three women in the picture; they're holding their coat collars closed, so it must have been cold . . .

HARRIET: Why would they make them scrub with toothbrushes?

SYLVIA, *angered:* To humiliate them, to make fools of them!

HARRIET: Oh!

SYLVIA: How can you be so . . . so . . . ? *Breaks off before she goes too far.* Harriet, please . . . leave me alone, will you?

HARRIET: This is not normal. Murray says the same thing. I swear to God, he came home last night and says. "She's got to stop thinking about those Germans." And you know how he loves current events. *Sylvia is staring ahead.* I'll see if the duck looks good, if not I'll get chops. Can I get you something now?

SYLVIA: No, I'm fine thanks.

HARRIET: I'm going. *Moves upstage of Sylvia.*

SYLVIA: Yes.

Sylvia returns to her paper. Harriet watches anxiously for a moment, out of Sylvia's sight line, then exits. Sylvia turns a page, absorbed in the paper. Suddenly she turns in shock—Phillip is standing behind her. He holds a small paper bag.

Oh! I didn't hear you come in.

GELLBURG: I tiptoed, in case you were dozing off . . . *His dour smile.* I bought you some sour pickles.

SYLVIA: Oh, that's nice! Later maybe. You have one.

GELLBURG: I'll wait. *Awkwardly but determined.* I was passing Greenberg's on Flatbush Avenue and I suddenly remembered how you used to love them. Remember?

SYLVIA: Thanks, that's nice of you. What were you doing on Flatbush Avenue?

GELLBURG: There's a property across from A&S. I'm probably going to foreclose.

SYLVIA: Oh that's sad. Are they nice people?

GELLBURG, *shrugs:* People are people—I gave them two extensions but they'll never manage . . . nothing up here. *Taps his temple.*

SYLVIA: Aren't you early?

GELLBURG: I got worried about you. Doctor come?

SYLVIA: He called; he has results of the tests but he wants to come tomorrow when he has more time to talk to me. He's really very nice.

GELLBURG: How was it today?

SYLVIA: I'm so sorry about this.

GELLBURG: You'll get better, don't worry about it. Oh! —There's a letter from the Captain. *Takes letter out of his jacket pocket.*

SYLVIA: Jerome?

GELLBURG, *terrific personal pride:* Read it.

His purse-mouthed grin is intense.

That's your son. General MacArthur *talked* to him twice.

SYLVIA: Fort Sill?

GELLBURG: Oklahoma. *He's going to lecture them on artillery!* In *Fort Sill!* That's the field artillery center. *She looks up dumbly.* That's like being invited to the Vatican to lecture the Pope.

SYLVIA: Imagine. *She folds the letter and hands it back to him.*

GELLBURG, *restraining greater resentment:* I don't understand this attitude.

SYLVIA: Why? I'm happy for him.

GELLBURG: You don't seem happy to me.

SYLVIA: I'll never get used to it. Who goes in the Army? Men who can't do anything else.

GELLBURG: I wanted people to see that a Jew doesn't have to be a lawyer or a doctor or a businessman.

SYLVIA: That's fine, but why must it be Jerome?

GELLBURG: For a Jewish boy, West Point is an honor. Without Mr. Case's connections, he'd never have gotten in. He could be the first Jewish General in the United States Army. Doesn't it mean something to be his mother?

SYLVIA, *with an edge of resentment:* Well, I said I'm glad.

GELLBURG: Don't be upset. *Looks about impatiently.* You know, when you get on your feet I'll help you hang the new drapes.

SYLVIA: I started to . . .

GELLBURG: But they've been here over a month.

SYLVIA: Well this happened, I'm sorry.

GELLBURG: You have to occupy yourself is all I'm saying, Sylvia, you can't give in to this.

SYLVIA, *near an outbreak:* Well I'm sorry—I'm sorry about everything!

GELLBURG: Please, don't get upset, I take it back!

A moment; stalemate.

SYLVIA: I wonder what my tests show.

Gellburg is silent.

That the specialist did.

GELLBURG: I went to see Dr. Hyman last night.

SYLVIA: You did? Why didn't you mention it?

GELLBURG: I wanted to think over what he said.

SYLVIA: What did he say?

With a certain deliberateness he goes over to her and gives her a kiss on the cheek. She is embarrassed and vaguely alarmed.

Phillip! *A little uncomprehending laugh.*

GELLBURG: I want to change some things. About the way I've been doing.

He stands there for a moment perfectly still, then rolls her chair closer to the upholstered chair in which he now sits and takes her hand. She doesn't quite know what to make of this, but doesn't remove her hand.

SYLVIA: Well what did he say?

GELLBURG, *he pats her hand:* I'll tell you in a minute. I'm thinking about a Dodge.

SYLVIA: A Dodge?

GELLBURG: I want to teach you to drive. So you can go where you like, visit your mother in the afternoon. —I want you to be happy, Sylvia.

SYLVIA, *surprised:* Oh.

GELLBURG: We have the money, we could do a lot of things. Maybe see Washington, D.C. . . . . It's supposed to be a very strong car, you know.

SYLVIA: But aren't they all black?—Dodges?

GELLBURG: Not all. I've seen a couple of green ones.

SYLVIA: You like green?

GELLBURG: It's only a color. You'll get used to it. —Or Chicago. It's really a big city, you know.

SYLVIA: Tell me what Doctor Hyman said.

GELLBURG, *gets himself set:* He thinks it could all be coming from your mind. Like a . . . a fear of some kind got into you. Psychological.

Sylvia is still, listening.

Are you afraid of something?

SYLVIA, *a slow shrug, a shake of her head:* . . . I don't know, I don't think so. What kind of fear, what does he mean?

GELLBURG: Well, he explains it better, but . . . like in a war, people get so afraid they go blind temporarily. What they call shell-shock. But once they feel safer it goes away.

SYLVIA, *thinks about this a moment:* What about the tests the Mt. Sinai man did?

GELLBURG: They can't find anything wrong with your body.

SYLVIA: But I'm numb!

GELLBURG: He claims being very frightened could be doing it. —Are you?

SYLVIA: I don't know.

GELLBURG: Personally . . . can I tell you what I think?

SYLVIA: What.

GELLBURG: I think it's this whole Nazi business.

SYLVIA: But it's in the paper—they're smashing up the Jewish stores
. . . should I not read the paper? The streets are covered with
broken glass!

GELLBURG: Yes, but you don't have to be constantly . . .

SYLVIA: It's ridiculous. I can't move my legs from reading a newspaper?

GELLBURG: He didn't say that; but I'm wondering if you're too involved with . . .

SYLVIA: It's ridiculous.

GELLBURG: Well, you talk to him tomorrow. *Pause—He comes back to
her and takes her hand, his need open.* You've got to get better,
Sylvia.

SYLVIA, *she sees his tortured face and tries to laugh:* What is this, am I
dying or something?

GELLBURG: How can you say that?

SYLVIA: I've never seen such a look in your face.

GELLBURG: Oh no-no-no . . . I'm just worried.

SYLVIA: I don't understand what's happening . . . *She turns away on
the verge of tears.*

GELLBURG: . . . I never realized . . . *Sudden sharpness* . . . look
at me, will you?

She turns to him; he glances down at the floor.

I wouldn't know what to do without you, Sylvia, honest to God. I
. . . *Immense difficulty.* I love you.

SYLVIA, *a dead, bewildered laugh:* What is this?

GELLBURG: You have to get better. If I'm ever doing something wrong I'll change it. Let's try to be different. All right? And you too, you've got to do what the doctors tell you.

SYLVIA: What can I do? Here I sit and they say there's nothing wrong with me.

GELLBURG: Listen . . . I think Hyman is a very smart man . . . *He lifts her hand and kisses her knuckles; embarrassed and smiling.* When we were talking, something came to mind; that maybe if we could sit down with him, the three of us, and maybe talk about . . . you know . . . everything.

Pause.

SYLVIA: That doesn't matter anymore, Phillip.

GELLBURG, *an embarrassed grin:* How do you know? Maybe . . .

SYLVIA: It's too late for that.

GELLBURG, *once launched he is terrified:* Why? Why is it too late?

SYLVIA: I'm surprised you're still worried about it.

GELLBURG: I'm not worried, I just think about it now and then.

SYLVIA: Well, it's too late, dear, it doesn't matter anymore, it hasn't for years. *She draws back her hand.*

Pause.

GELLBURG: . . . Well, all right. But if you wanted to I'd . . .

SYLVIA: We did talk about it, I took you to Rabbi Steiner about it twice, what good did it do?

GELLBURG: In those days I still thought it would change by itself. I was so young, I didn't understand such things. It came out of nowhere and I thought it would go the same way.

SYLVIA: I'm sorry, Phillip, it didn't come out of nowhere.

Silent, Gellburg evades her eyes.

You regretted you got married.

GELLBURG: I didn't "regret it" . . .

SYLVIA: You did, dear. You don't have to be ashamed of it.

A long silence.

GELLBURG: I'm going to tell you the truth—in those days I thought that if we separated I wouldn't die of it. I admit that.

SYLVIA: I always knew that.

GELLBURG: But I haven't felt that way in years now.

SYLVIA: Well, I'm here. *Spreads her arms out, a wildly ironical look in her eyes.* Here I am, Phillip!

GELLBURG, *offended:* The way you say that is not very . . .

SYLVIA: Not very what? I'm here; I've been here a long time.

GELLBURG, *a helpless surge of anger:* I'm trying to tell you something!

SYLVIA, *openly taunting him now:* But I said I'm here!

Gellburg moves about as she speaks, as though trying to find an escape or a way in.

I'm here for my mother's sake, and Jerome's sake and everybody's sake except mine, but I'm here and here I am. And now finally you want to talk about it, now when I'm turning into an old woman? How do you want me to say it? Tell me, dear, I'll say it the way you want me to. What should I say?

GELLBURG, *insulted and guilty:* I want you to stand up.

SYLVIA: I can't stand up.

Gellburg takes both her hands.

GELLBURG: You can. Now come on. Stand up.

SYLVIA: I can't!

GELLBURG: You can stand up, Sylvia. Now lean to me and get on your feet.

He pulls her up; then steps aside releasing her; she collapses on the floor. He stands over her.

What are you trying to do? *He goes to his knees to yell into her face. What are you trying to do, Sylvia!*

She looks at him in terror at the mystery before her.

Blackout.

SCENE THREE

The lone cellist plays. Then lights go down.

Dr. Hyman's office. He is in riding clothes. Hyman is seated beside his desk.

HARRIET: My poor sister. And they have everything! But how can it be in the mind if she's so paralyzed?

HYMAN: Her numbness is random, it doesn't follow the nerve paths; only part of the thighs are affected, part of the calves, it makes no physiological sense. I have a few things I'd like to ask you, all right?

HARRIET: You know, I'm glad it's you taking care of her, my husband says the same thing.

HYMAN: Thank you . . .

HARRIET: You probably don't remember, but you once took out our cousin, Roslyn Fein? She said you were great.

HYMAN: Roslyn Fein. When?

HARRIET: She's very tall and reddish blond hair? She had a real crush . . .

HYMAN, *pleased:* When was this?

HARRIET: Oh—NYU, maybe twenty-five years ago. She adored you; seriously, she said you were really *great. Laughs knowingly.* Used to take her to Coney Island swimming, and so on.

HYMAN, *laughs with her:* Oh. Well, give her my regards.

HARRIET: I hardly see her, she lives in Florida.

HYMAN, *pressing on:* I'd like you to tell me about Sylvia; —before she collapsed, was there any sign of some shock, or anything? Something threatening her?

HARRIET, *thinks for a moment, shrugs, shaking her head:* Listen, I'll tell you something funny—to me sometimes she seems . . . I was going to say happy, but it's more like . . . I don't know . . . like this is how she wants to be. I mean since the collapse. Don't you think so?

HYMAN: Well I never really knew her before. What about this fascination with the Nazis—she ever talk to you about that?

HARRIET: Only this last couple of weeks. I don't understand it, they're in *Germany,* how can she be so frightened, it's across the ocean, isn't it?

HYMAN: Yes. But in a way it isn't. *He stares, shaking his head, lost* . . . She's very sensitive; she really sees the people in those photographs. They're alive to her.

HARRIET, *suddenly near tears:* My poor sister!

HYMAN: Tell me about Phillip.

HARRIET: Phillip? *Shrugs.* Phillip is Phillip.

HYMAN: You like him?

HARRIET: Well, he's my brother-in-law . . . You mean personally?

HYMAN: Yes.

HARRIET, *takes a breath to lie:* . . . He can be very sweet, you know. But suddenly he'll turn around and talk to you like you've got four legs and long ears. The men—not that they don't respect him—but they'd just as soon not play cards with him if they can help it.

HYMAN: Really. Why?

HARRIET: Well, God forbid you have an opinion—you open your mouth and he gives you that Republican look down his nose and your brains dry up. Not that I don't *like* him . . .

HYMAN: How did he and Sylvia meet?

HARRIET: She was head bookkeeper at Empire Steel over there in Long Island City . . .

HYMAN: She must have been very young.

HARRIET: . . . Twenty; just out of high school practically and she's head bookkeeper. According to my husband God gave Sylvia all the brains and the rest of us the big feet! The reason they met was the company took out a mortgage and she had to explain all the accounts to Phillip—he used to say "I fell in love with her figures!" *Hyman laughs.* Why should I lie? —Personally to me, he's a little bit a prune. Like he never stops with the whole Jewish part of it.

HYMAN: He doesn't like being Jewish.

HARRIET: Well yes and no—like Jerome being the only Jewish Captain, he's proud of that. And him being the only one ever worked for Brooklyn Guarantee—he's proud of that too, but at the same time . . .

HYMAN: . . . He'd rather not be one.

HARRIET: . . . Look, he's a mystery to me. I don't understand him and I never will.

HYMAN: What about the marriage? I promise you this is strictly between us.

HARRIET: What can I tell you, the marriage is a marriage.

HYMAN: And?

HARRIET: I shouldn't talk about it.

HYMAN: It stays in this office. Tell me. They ever break up?

HARRIET: Oh God no! Why should they? He's a wonderful provider. There's no Depression for Phillip, you know. And it would kill our mother, she worships Phillip, she'd never outlive it. No-no, it's out of the question, Sylvia's not that kind of woman, although . . . *Breaks off.*

HYMAN: Come, Harriet, I need to know these things.

HARRIET: . . . Well, I guess everybody knows it so . . . *Takes a breath.* I think they came very close to it one time . . . when he hit her with the steak.

HYMAN: Hit her with a *steak?*

HARRIET: It was overdone.

HYMAN: What do you mean, hit her?

HARRIET: He picked it up off the plate and slapped her in the face with it.

HYMAN: And then what?

HARRIET: Well if my mother hadn't patched it up I don't know what would have happened, and then he went out and bought her that gorgeous beaver coat, and repainted the whole house, and he's tight as a drum, you know, so it was hard for him. I don't know what to tell you. —Why? —You think *he* could have frightened her like this?

HYMAN, *hesitates:* I don't know yet. The whole thing is very strange.

Something darkens her expression and she begins to shake her head from side to side and she bursts into tears. He comes and puts an arm around her.

What is it?

HARRIET: All her life she did nothing but love everybody!

HYMAN, *reaches out to take her hand:* Harriet.

She looks at him.

What do you want to tell me?

HARRIET: I don't know if it's right to talk about. But of course, it's years and years ago . . .

HYMAN: None of this will ever be repeated; believe me.

HARRIET: Well . . . every first-of-the-year when Uncle Myron was still alive we'd all go down to his basement for a New Year's party. I'm talking like fifteen, sixteen years ago. He's dead now, Myron, but . . . he was . . . you know . . . *Small laugh* . . . a little comical; he always kept this shoe box full of . . . you know, these postcards.

HYMAN: You mean . . .

HARRIET: Yes. French. You know, naked women, and men with these great big . . . you know . . . they hung down like salamis. And everybody'd pass them around and die laughing. It was exactly the same thing every New Year's. But this time, all of a sudden, Phillip . . . we thought he'd lost his mind . . .

HYMAN: What happened?

HARRIET: Well Sylvia's in the middle of laughing and he grabs the postcard out of her hand and he turns around screaming—I mean, really screaming—that we're all a bunch of morons and idiots and God knows what and takes hold of her and throws her up the stairs. Bang! It cracked the bannister, I can still hear it. *Catches her breath.* I tell you it was months before anybody'd talk to him again. Because everybody on the block loves Sylvia.

HYMAN: What do you suppose made him do that?

HARRIET, *shrugs:* . . . Well, if you listen to some of the men—but of course some of the dirty minds on this block . . . if you spread it over the back yard you'd get tomatoes six feet high.

HYMAN: Why? —What'd they say?

HARRIET: Well, that the reason he got so mad was because he couldn't . . . you know . . .

HYMAN: Oh, really.

HARRIET: . . . Anymore.

HYMAN: But they made up.

HARRIET: Listen, to be truthful you have to say it—although it'll sound crazy . . .

HYMAN: What.

HARRIET: You watch him sometimes when they've got people over and she's talking—he'll sit quietly in the corner, and the expression on that man's face when he's watching her—it could almost break your heart.

HYMAN: Why?

HARRIET: He adores her!

Blackout.

SCENE FOUR

The cellist plays, and is gone.

Stanton Case is getting ready to leave his office. Putting on his blazer and a captain's cap and a foulard. Gellburg enters.

CASE: Good! —You're back. I was just leaving.

GELLBURG: I'm sorry, I got caught in traffic over in Crown Heights.

CASE: I wanted to talk to you again about 611. Sit down for a moment.

Both sit.

We're sailing out through the Narrows in about an hour.

GELLBURG: Beautiful day for it.

CASE: Are you all right? You don't look well.

GELLBURG: Oh no, I'm fine.

CASE: Good. Have you come to anything final on 611. I like the price, I can tell you that right off.

GELLBURG: Yes, the price is good, but I'm still . . .

CASE: I've walked past it again; I think with some renovation it would make a fine annex for the Harvard Club.

GELLBURG: It's a very nice structure, yes. I'm not final on it yet but I have a few comments . . . unless you've got to get on the water right away.

CASE: I have a few minutes. Go ahead.

GELLBURG: . . . Before I forget—we got a very nice letter from Jerome.

No reaction from Case.

My boy.

CASE: Oh yes! —How is he doing?

GELLBURG: They're bringing him out to Fort Sill . . . some kind of lecture on artillery.

CASE: Really now! Well isn't that nice! . . . Then he's really intending to make a career in the Army.

GELLBURG, *surprised Case isn't aware:* Oh absolutely.

CASE: Well that's good, isn't it. It's quite surprising for one of you people—for some reason I'd assumed he just wanted the education.

GELLBURG: Oh no. It's his life. I'll never know how to thank you.

CASE: No trouble at all. The Point can probably use a few of you people to keep the rest of them awake. Now what's this about 611?

GELLBURG, *sets himself in all dignity:* You might recall, we used the ABC Plumbing Contractors on a couple of buildings?

CASE: ABC? —I don't recall. What have they got to do with it?

GELLBURG: They're located in the neighborhood, just off Broadway, and on a long shot I went over to see Mr. Liebfreund—he runs ABC. I was wondering if they may have done any work for Wanamaker's.

CASE: Wanamaker's! What's Wanamaker's got to do with it?

GELLBURG: I buy my shirts in Wanamaker's, and last time I was in there I caught my shoe on a splinter sticking up out of the floor.

CASE: Well that store is probably fifty years old . . .

GELLBURG: Closer to seventy-five. I tripped and almost fell down; this was very remarkable to me, that they would leave a floor in such condition. So I began wondering about it . . .

CASE: About what?

GELLBURG: Number 611 is two blocks from Wanamaker's. *A little extra-wise grin.* They're the biggest business in the area, a whole square block, after all. Anyway, sure enough, turns out ABC does all Wanamaker's plumbing work. And Liebfreund tells me he's had to keep patching up their boilers *because they canceled installation of new boilers last winter.* A permanent cancellation.

Pause.

CASE: And what do you make of that?

GELLBURG: I think it could mean they're either moving the store, or maybe going out of business.

CASE: *Wanamaker's?*

GELLBURG: It's possible, I understand the family is practically died out. Either way, if Wanamaker's disappears, Mr. Case, that neighborhood in my opinion is no longer prime. Also, I called Kevin Sullivan over at Title Guarantee and he says they turned down 611 last year and he can't remember why.

CASE: Then what are you telling me?

GELLBURG: I would not touch Number 611 with a ten-foot pole. If that neighborhood starts to slide 611 is a great big slice of lemon.

CASE: Well. That's very disappointing. It would have made a wonderful club annex.

GELLBURG: With a thing like the Harvard Club you have got to think of the far distant future, Mr. Case, I don't have to tell you that, and the future of that part of Broadway is a definite possible negative. *Raising a monitory finger.*—I emphasize "possible," mind you; only God can predict.

CASE: Well I must say, I would never have thought of Wanamaker's disappearing. You've been more than thorough, Gellburg, we appreciate it. I've got to run now, but we'll talk about this further . . . *Glances at his watch.* Mustn't miss the tide . . . *Moves, indicates.* Take a brandy if you like . . . Wife all right?

GELLBURG: Oh yes, she's fine!

CASE, *the faint shadow of a warning:* Sure everything's all right with you—we don't want you getting sick now.

GELLBURG: Oh no, I'm very well, very well.

CASE: I'll be back on Monday, we'll go into this further. *Indicates.* Take a brandy if you like.

GELLBURG: Yes, sir, I might!

Case exits rather jauntily. Gellburg stands alone; his hands come up and he tries to rub some color into his suffering face.

Blackout.

SCENE FIVE

The cello plays and the music falls away.

Sylvia in bed, reading a book. She looks up as Hyman enters. He is in his riding clothes. Sylvia has a certain excitement at seeing him.

SYLVIA: Oh, Doctor!

HYMAN: I let myself in, hope I didn't scare you . . .

SYLVIA: Oh no, I'm glad. Sit down. You been riding?

HYMAN: Yes. All the way down to Brighton Beach, nice long ride. —I expected to see you jumping rope by now. *Sylvia laughs, embarrassed.* I think you're just trying to get out of doing the dishes.

SYLVIA, *strained laugh:* Oh stop. You really love riding, don't you?

HYMAN: Well, there's no telephone on a horse.

Sylvia laughs.

   Ocean Parkway is like a German forest this time of the morning— riding under that archway of maple trees is like poetry.

SYLVIA: Wonderful. I never did anything like that.

HYMAN: Well, let's go —I'll take you out and teach you sometime. Have you been trying the exercise?

SYLVIA: I can't do it.

HYMAN, *shaking a finger at Sylvia:* You've got to do it, Sylvia. You could end up permanently crippled. Let's have a look.

He sits on the bed and draws the cover off her legs, then raises her nightgown. She inhales with a certain anticipation as he does so. He feels her toes.

You feel this at all?

SYLVIA: Well . . . not really.

HYMAN: I'm going to pinch your toe. Ready?

SYLVIA: All right.

He pinches her big toe sharply; she doesn't react. He rests a palm on her leg.

HYMAN: Your skin feels a little too cool. You're going to lose your muscle tone if you don't move. Your legs will begin to lose volume and shrink . . .

SYLVIA, *tears threaten:* I know . . . !

HYMAN: And look what beautiful legs you have, Sylvia. I'm afraid you're getting comfortable in this condition . . .

SYLVIA: I'm not. I keep trying to move them . . .

HYMAN: But look now—here it's eleven in the morning and you're happily tucked into bed like it's midnight.

SYLVIA: But I've tried . . . ! Are you really sure it's not a virus of some kind?

HYMAN: There's nothing. Sylvia, you have a strong beautiful body . . .

SYLVIA: But what can I do, I can't feel anything!

She sits up with her face raised to him; he starts to cup it in his hand, but stands and moves abruptly away. Then turning back to her . . .

HYMAN: I really should find someone else for you.

SYLVIA: Why! —I don't want anyone else!

HYMAN: You're a very attractive woman, don't you know that?

SYLVIA, *deeply excited, glancing away shyly:* . . . Well, you mustn't get anyone else.

HYMAN: Sylvia, listen to me . . . I haven't been this moved by a woman in a very long time. *He touches her hair.* Tell me the truth, Sylvia. Sylvia? How did this happen to you?

SYLVIA, *she avoids his gaze:* I don't know. *Sylvia's anxiety rises as he speaks now.*

HYMAN: . . . I'm going to be straight with you; I thought this was going to be simpler than it's turning out to be, and I care about you too much to play a game with your health. I can't deny my vanity, I have a lot of it, but I have to face it—I know you want to tell me something and I don't know how to get it out of you. *Sylvia covers her face, ashamed.* You're a responsible woman, Sylvia, you have to start helping me, you can't just lie there and expect a miracle to lift you to your feet. You tell me now—what should I know?

SYLVIA: I would tell you if I knew! *Hyman turns away defeated and impatient.* Couldn't we just talk and maybe I could . . . *Breaks off.* I like you. A lot. I love when you talk to me . . . couldn't we just . . . like for a few minutes. . . .

HYMAN: Okay. What do you want to talk about?

SYLVIA: Please. Be patient. I'm . . . I'm trying. *Relieved; a fresher mood.* Harriet says you used to take out our cousin Roslyn Fein.

HYMAN: It's possible, I don't remember.

SYLVIA: Well, you had so many, didn't you.

HYMAN: When I was younger.

SYLVIA: Roslyn said you used to do acrobatics on the beach? And all the girls would stand around going crazy for you.

HYMAN: That's a long time ago . . .

SYLVIA: And you'd take them under the boardwalk. *Laughs.*

HYMAN: Nobody had money for anything else. Didn't you used to go to the beach?

SYLVIA: Sure. But I never did anything like that.

HYMAN: You must have been very shy.

SYLVIA: I guess, but I had to look out for my sisters, being the eldest . . .

HYMAN: Can we talk about Phillip?

Caught unaware, her eyes show fear.

I'd really like to, unless you . . .

SYLVIA, *challenged:* No! —It's all right.

HYMAN: . . . Are you afraid right now?

SYLVIA: No, not . . . Yes. *Picks up the book beside her.* Have you read Anthony Adverse?

HYMAN: No, but I hear it's sold a million copies.

SYLVIA: It's wonderful. I rent it from Womraths.

HYMAN: Was Phillip your first boyfriend?

SYLVIA: The first serious.

HYMAN: He's a fine man.

SYLVIA: Yes, he is.

HYMAN: Is he interesting to be with?

SYLVIA: Interesting?

HYMAN: Do you have things to talk about?

SYLVIA: Well . . . business, mostly. I was head bookkeeper for Empire Steel in Long Island City . . . years ago, when we met, I mean.

HYMAN: He didn't want you to work?

SYLVIA: No.

HYMAN: I imagine you were a good business woman.

SYLVIA: Oh, I loved it! I've always enjoyed . . . you know, people depending on me.

HYMAN: Yes. —Do I frighten you talking like this?

SYLVIA: A little. —But I want you to.

HYMAN: Why?

SYLVIA: I don't know. You make me feel . . . hopeful.

HYMAN: You mean of getting better?

SYLVIA:—Of myself. Of getting . . . *Breaks off.*

HYMAN: Getting what?

Sylvia shakes her head, refusing to go on.

. . . Free?

Sylvia suddenly kisses the palm of his hand. He wipes her hair away from her eyes. He stands up and walks a few steps away.

I want you to raise your knees.

Sylvia doesn't move.

Come, bring up your knees.

SYLVIA, *she tries:* I can't!

HYMAN: You can. I want you to send your thoughts into your hips. Tense your hips. Think of the bones in your hips. Come on now. The strongest muscles in your body are right there, you still have tremendous power there. Tense your hips. *She is tensing.* Now tense your thighs. Those are long dense muscles with tremendous power. Do it, draw up your knees. Come on, raise your knees. Keep it up. Concentrate. Raise it. Do it for me. *With an exhaled gasp she gives up. Remaining yards away . . .* Your body strength must be marvelous. The depth of your flesh must be wonderful. Why are you cut off from yourself? You should be dancing, you should be stretching out in the sun . . . Sylvia, I know you know more than you're saying, why can't you open up to me? Speak to me. Sylvia? Say anything. *Sylvia looks at him in silence.* I promise I won't tell a soul. What is in your mind right now. *A pause.*

SYLVIA: Tell me about Germany.

HYMAN, *surprised:* Germany. Why Germany?

SYLVIA: Why did you go there to study?

HYMAN: The American medical schools have quotas on Jews, I would have had to wait for years and maybe never get in.

SYLVIA: But they hate Jews there, don't they?

HYMAN: These Nazis can't possibly last— Why are you so preoccupied with them?

SYLVIA: I don't know. But when I saw that picture in the *Times*—with those two old men on their knees in the street . . . *Presses her ears.* I swear, I almost heard that crowd laughing, and ridiculing them. —I don't know what happened, Phillip never wants to talk about being Jewish, except—you know—to joke about it sometimes the way people do. But all this Nazi business—it's hard to talk to anybody about it, not just Phillip. They just don't want to hear it.

HYMAN: What would you like to say to Phillip about it?

SYLVIA, *with an empty laugh, a head shake:* I don't even know! Just to talk about it . . . it's almost like there's something in me that . . . it's silly . . .

HYMAN: No, it's interesting. What do you mean, something in you?

SYLVIA: I have no word for it, I don't know what I'm saying, it's like . . . *She presses her chest.*—something alive, like a child almost, except it's a very dark thing . . . and it frightens me! *Hyman moves his hand to calm her and she grabs it.*

HYMAN: That was hard to say, wasn't it. *Sylvia nods.* You have a lot of courage. —We'll talk more, but I want you to try something now. I'll stand here, and I want you to imagine something. *Sylvia turns to him, curious.* I want you to imagine that we've made love. *Startled, she laughs tensely. He joins this laugh.* I've made love to you. And now it's over and we are lying together. And you begin to tell me some secret things. Things that are way down deep on your heart. *Slight pause.* Sylvia— *Hyman comes around the bed, bends and kisses her.* Tell me about Phillip. *Sylvia is silent, does not grasp his head to hold him. He straightens up.* Think about it. We'll talk tomorrow again. Okay?

Hyman exits. Sylvia lies there inert for a moment. Then she tenses with effort, trying to raise her knee. It doesn't work. She reaches down and lifts the knee, and then the other and lies there that way. Then she lets her knees spread apart . . .

Blackout.

SCENE SIX

The cellist plays, then is gone.

Hyman's office. Gellburg is sitting. Immediately Margaret enters with a cup of cocoa, cup of tea and a file folder. She hands the cup of cocoa to Gellburg.

GELLBURG: Cocoa?

MARGARET: I drink a lot of it, it calms the nerves. Have you lost weight?

GELLBURG, *impatience with her prying:* A little, I think.

MARGARET: Did you always sigh so much?

GELLBURG: Sigh?

MARGARET: You probably don't realize you're doing it. You should have him listen to your heart.

GELLBURG: No-no, I think I'm alright. *Sighs.* I guess I've always sighed. Is that a sign of something?

MARGARET: Not necessarily; but ask Harry. He's just finishing with a patient. —There's no change, I understand.

GELLBURG: No, she's the same. *Impatiently hands her the cup.* I can't drink this.

MARGARET: Are you eating at all?

GELLBURG, *suddenly shifting his mode:* I came to talk to *him.*

MARGARET, *sharply:* I was only trying to be helpful!

GELLBURG: I'm kind of upset, I didn't mean any . . .

Hyman enters, surprising her. She exits, insulted.

HYMAN: I'm sorry. But she means well.

Gellburg silently nods, irritation intact.

It won't happen again. *He takes his seat.* I have to admit, though, she has a very good diagnostic sense. Women are more instinctive sometimes . . .

GELLBURG: Excuse me, I don't come here to be talking to her.

HYMAN, *a kidding laugh:* Oh, come on, Phillip, take it easy. What's Sylvia doing?

GELLBURG, *it takes him a moment to compose:* . . . I don't know what she's doing.

Hyman waits. Gellburg has a tortured look; now he seems to brace himself, and faces the Doctor with what seems a haughty air.

I decided to try to do what you advised. —About the loving.

HYMAN: . . . Yes?

GELLBURG: So I decided to try to do it with her.

HYMAN: . . . Sex?

GELLBURG: What then, handball? Of course sex.

The openness of this hostility mystifies Hyman who becomes apologetic.

HYMAN: . . . Well, do you mean you've done it or you're going to?

GELLBURG, *long pause; he seems not to be sure he wants to continue. Now he sounds reasonable again:* You see, we haven't been really . . . together. For . . . quite a long time. *Correcting.* I mean specially since this started to happen.

HYMAN: You mean the last two weeks.

GELLBURG: Well yes. *Great discomfort.* And some time before that.

HYMAN: I see. *But he desists from asking how long a time before that. A pause.*

GELLBURG: So I thought maybe it would help her if . . . you know.

HYMAN: Yes, I think the warmth would help. In fact, to be candid, Phillip—I'm beginning to wonder if this whole fear of the Nazis isn't because she feels . . . extremely vulnerable; I'm in no sense trying to blame you, but . . . a woman who doesn't feel loved can get very disoriented, you know?—lost. *Hyman has noticed a strangeness.*—Something wrong?

GELLBURG: She says she's not being loved?

HYMAN: No-no, I'm talking about how she may feel.

GELLBURG: Listen . . . *Struggles for a moment; now, firmly.* I'm wondering if you could put me in touch with somebody.

HYMAN: You mean for yourself?

GELLBURG: I don't know; I'm not sure what they do, though.

HYMAN: I know a very good man at the hospital, if you want me to set it up.

GELLBURG: Well, maybe not yet, let me let you know.

HYMAN: Sure.

GELLBURG: Your wife says I sigh a lot. Does that mean something?

HYMAN: Could just be tension. Come in when you have a little time, I'll look you over . . . Am I wrong? —You sound like something's happened . . .

GELLBURG: This whole thing is against me . . . *Attempting a knowing grin.* But you know that.

HYMAN: Now wait a minute . . .

GELLBURG: She knows what she's doing, you're not blind.

HYMAN: What happened, why are you saying this?

GELLBURG: I was late last night—I had to be in Jersey all afternoon, a problem we have there—she was sound asleep. So I made myself some spaghetti. Usually she puts something out for me.

HYMAN: She has no problem cooking.

GELLBURG: I told you—she gets around the kitchen fine in the wheelchair. Flora shops in the morning—that's the maid. Although I'm beginning to wonder if Sylvia gets out and walks around when I leave the house.

HYMAN: It's impossible. —She is paralyzed, Phillip, it's not a trick— she's suffering.

GELLBURG, *a sideways glance at Hyman:* What do you discuss with her? —You know, she talks like you see right through her.

HYMAN, *a laugh:* I wish I could! We talk about getting her to walk, that's all. This thing is not against you, Phillip, believe me. *Slight laugh.*—I wish you could trust me, kid!

GELLBURG, *momentarily on the edge of being reassured, he studies Hyman's face for a moment, nodding very slightly:* I would never believe I could talk this way to another person. I do trust you.

Pause.

HYMAN: Good!—I'm listening, go ahead.

GELLBURG: The first time we talked you asked me if we . . . how many times a week.

HYMAN: Yes.

GELLBURG, *nods:* . . . I have a problem sometimes.

HYMAN: Oh. —Well, that's fairly common, you know.

GELLBURG, *relieved:* You see it often?

HYMAN: Oh very often, yes.

GELLBURG, *a tense challenging smile:* Ever happen to you?

HYMAN, *surprised:* . . . Me? Well sure, a few times. Is this something recent?

GELLBURG: Well . . . yes. Recent and also . . . *Breaks off, indicating the past with a gesture of his hand.*

HYMAN: I see. It doesn't help if you're under tension, you know.

GELLBURG: Yes, I was wondering that.

HYMAN: Just don't start thinking it's the end of the world because it's not—you're still a young man. Think of it like the ocean—it goes out but it always comes in again. But the thing to keep in mind is that she loves you and wants you.

Gellburg looks wide eyed.

You know that, don't you?

GELLBURG, *silently nods for an instant:* My sister-in-law Harriet says you were a real hotshot on the beach years ago.

HYMAN: Years ago, yes.

GELLBURG: I used to wonder if it's because Sylvia's the only one I was ever with.

HYMAN: Why would that matter?

GELLBURG: I don't know exactly—it used to prey on my mind that . . . maybe she expected more.

HYMAN: Yes. Well, that's a common idea, you know. In fact, some men take on a lot of women not out of confidence but because they're afraid to lose it.

GELLBURG, *fascinated:* Huh! I'd never of thought of that. —A doctor must get a lot of peculiar cases, I bet.

HYMAN, *with utter intimacy:* Everybody's peculiar in one way or another but I'm not here to judge people. Why don't you try to tell me what happened? *His grin; making light of it.* Come on, give it a shot.

GELLBURG: All right . . . *Sighs.* I get into bed. She's sound asleep . . . *Breaks off. Resumes; something transcendent seems to enter him.* Nothing like it ever happened to me, I got a . . . a big yen for her. She's even more beautiful when she sleeps. I gave her a kiss. On the mouth. She didn't wake up. I never had such a yen in my life.

Long pause.

HYMAN: And?

Gellburg silent.

Did you make love?

GELLBURG: . . . Yes.

HYMAN, *a quickening. Something tentative in Gellburg mystifies:* . . .
How did she react? —It's been some time since you did it, you
say.

GELLBURG: Well, yes.

HYMAN: Then what was the reaction?

GELLBURG: She was . . . *searches for the word.* gasping. It was
really something. I thought of what you told me—about loving
her now; I felt I'd brought her out of it. I was almost sure of it.
She was like a different woman than I ever knew.

HYMAN: That's wonderful. Did she move her legs?

GELLBURG, *unprepared for that question:* . . . I think so.

HYMAN: Well did she or didn't she?

GELLBURG: Well I was so excited I didn't really notice, but I guess she
must have.

HYMAN: That's wonderful, why are you so upset?

GELLBURG: Well let me finish, there's more to it.

HYMAN: Sorry, go ahead.

GELLBURG: —I brought her some breakfast this morning and—you
know—started to—you know—talk a little about it. She looked at
me like I was crazy. She claims she doesn't remember doing it. It
never happened.

Hyman is silent, plays with a pen. Something evasive in this.

How could she not remember it?

HYMAN: You're sure she was awake?

GELLBURG: How could she not be?

HYMAN: Did she say anything during the . . . ?

GELLBURG: Well no, but she's never said much.

HYMAN: Did she open her eyes?

GELLBURG: I'm not sure. We were in the dark, but she usually keeps them closed. *Impatiently.* But she was . . . she was groaning, panting . . . she had to be awake! And now to say she doesn't remember?

Shaken, Hyman gets up and moves; a pause.

HYMAN: So what do you think is behind it?

GELLBURG: Well what would any man think? She's trying to turn me into nothing!

HYMAN: Now wait, you're jumping to conclusions.

GELLBURG: Is such a thing possible? I want your medical opinion— could a woman not remember?

HYMAN, *a moment, then . . . :* How did she look when she said that; did she seem sincere about not remembering?

GELLBURG: She looked like I was talking about something on the moon. Finally, she said a terrible thing. I still can't get over it.

HYMAN: What'd she say?

GELLBURG: That I'd imagined doing it.

Long pause. Hyman doesn't move.

What's your opinion? Well . . . could a man imagine such a thing? Is that possible?

HYMAN, *after a moment:* Tell you what; supposing I have another talk with her and see what I can figure out?

GELLBURG, *angrily demanding:* You have an opinion, don't you? —How could a man imagine such a thing!

HYMAN: I don't know what to say . . .

GELLBURG: What do you mean you don't know what to say! It's impossible, isn't it? To invent such a thing?

HYMAN, *fear of being out of his depth:* Phillip, don't cross-examine me, I'm doing everything I know to help you! —Frankly, I can't follow what you're telling me—you're sure in your own mind you had relations with her?

GELLBURG: How can you even ask me such a thing? Would I say it unless I was sure? *Stands, shaking with fear and anger.* I don't understand your attitude! *He starts out.*

HYMAN: Phillip, please! *In fear he intercepts Gellburg.* What attitude, what are you talking about?

GELLBURG: I'm going to vomit, I swear—I don't feel well . . .

HYMAN: What happened . . . has she said something about me?

GELLBURG: About you? What do you mean? What could she say?

HYMAN, *shouting:* I don't understand why you're so upset with me!

GELLBURG, *shouts:* What are you doing!

HYMAN, *guiltily:* What am *I* doing! What are you talking about!

GELLBURG: She is trying to destroy me! And you stand there! And what do you do! Are you a doctor or what! *He goes right up to Hyman's face.* Why don't you give me a straight answer about anything! Everything is in-and-out and around-the-block! —Listen, I've made up my mind; I don't want you seeing her anymore.

HYMAN: I think she's the one has to decide that.

GELLBURG: I am deciding it! It's decided!

Gellburg storms out. Hyman stands there guilty, alarmed. Margaret enters.

MARGARET: Now what? He gone off too? *Seeing Hyman's anxiety.* Why are you looking like that?

Hyman evasively returns to his desk chair.

Are *you* in trouble?

HYMAN: Me! Cut it out, will you?

MARGARET: Cut what out? I asked a question—are you?

HYMAN: I said to cut it out, Margaret!

MARGARET: I will never understand it. Except I do, I guess; you believe women. Woman tells you the earth is flat and for that five minutes you're swept away, helpless.

HYMAN, *laughs:* Nothing's happened. *Nothing has happened!* Why are you going on about it!

MARGARET: Because you don't realize how transparent you are. You're a pane of glass, Harry— Mrs. Gellburg has you by the short ones . . .

HYMAN: You know what baffles me?

MARGARET: . . . And it's irritating. —What is it—just new ass all the time? But what can be new about an ass?

HYMAN: There's been nobody for at least ten or twelve years . . . more! I can't remember anymore!

MARGARET: What baffles you?

HYMAN: Why I take your suspicions seriously.

MARGARET: Oh that's easy. —You love the truth, Harry.

HYMAN, *a deep sigh, facing upward:* I'm exhausted.

MARGARET: What about asking Charley Whitman to see her?

HYMAN: She's frightened to death of psychiatry, she thinks it means she's crazy.

MARGARET: Well, she is, in a way, isn't she?

HYMAN: I don't see it that way at all.

MARGARET: Getting this hysterical about something on the other side of the world is sane?

HYMAN: When she talks about it it's not the other side of the world, it's on the next block.

MARGARET: And that's sane?

HYMAN: I don't know what it is! I just get the feeling sometimes that she *knows* something, something that . . . It's like she's connected to some . . . some wire that goes half around the world, some truth that other people are blind to.

MARGARET: I think you've got to get somebody on this who won't be carried away, Harry.

HYMAN: I am not carried away!

MARGARET: You really believe that Sylvia Gellburg is being threatened by these Nazis? Is that real or is it hysterical?

HYMAN: So call it hysterical, does that bring you one inch closer to what is driving that woman? It's not a word that's driving her, Margaret—she *knows* something! I don't know what it is, and she may not either—but I tell you it's real.

A moment.

MARGARET: What an interesting life you have, Harry.

Blackout.

SCENE SEVEN

The cellist plays, music fades away.

Stanton Case is standing with hands clasped behind his back as though staring out a window. A dark mood. Gellburg enters behind him but he doesn't turn at once.

GELLBURG: Excuse me . . .

CASE, *turns:* Oh, good morning. You wanted to see me.

GELLBURG: If you have a minute, I'd appreciate . . .

CASE, *as he sits:* —You don't look well, are you alright?

GELLBURG: Oh I'm fine, maybe a cold coming on . . .

Since he hasn't been invited to sit he glances at a chair then back at Case who still leaves him hanging—and he sits on the chair's edge.

I wanted you to know how bad I feel about 611 Broadway. I'm very sorry.

CASE: Yes. Well. So it goes, I guess.

GELLBURG: I know you had your heart set on it and I . . . I tell you the news knocked me over; they gave no sign they were talking to Allen Kershowitz or anybody else . . .

CASE: It's very disappointing—in fact, I'd already begun talking to an architect friend about renovations.

GELLBURG: Really. Well, I can't tell you how . . .

CASE: I'd gotten a real affection for that building. It certainly would have made a perfect annex. And probably a great investment too.

GELLBURG: Well, not necessarily, if Wanamaker's ever pulls out.

CASE: . . . Yes, about Wanamaker's—I should tell you—when I found out that Kershowitz had outbid us I was flabbergasted after what you'd said about the neighborhood going downhill once the store was gone— Kershowitz is no fool, I need hardly say. So I mentioned it to one of our club members who I know is related to a member of the Wanamaker board. —He tells me there has never been any discussion whatever about the company moving out; he was simply amazed at the idea.

GELLBURG: But the man at ABC . . .

CASE, *impatience showing:* ABC lost their boiler work because Wanamaker's changed to another contractor three years ago. It had nothing to do with the store moving out. Nothing.

GELLBURG: . . . I don't know what to say, I . . . I just . . . I'm awfully sorry . . .

CASE: Well, it's a beautiful building, let's hope Kershowitz puts it to some worthwhile use. —You have any idea what he plans to do with it?

GELLBURG: Me? Oh no, I don't really know Kershowitz.

CASE: Oh! I thought you said you knew him for years?

GELLBURG: . . . Well, I "know" him, but not . . . we're not personal friends or anything, we just met at closing a few times, and things like that. And maybe once or twice in restaurants, I think, but . . .

CASE: I see. I guess I misunderstood, I thought you were fairly close.

Case says no more; the full stop shoots Gellburg's anxiety way up.

GELLBURG: I hope you're not . . . I mean I never mentioned to Kershowitz that you were interested in 611.

CASE: Mentioned? What do you mean?

GELLBURG: Nothing; just that . . . it almost sounds like I had something to do with him grabbing the building away from under you. Because I would never do a thing like that to you!

CASE: I didn't say that, did I. If I seem upset it's being screwed out of that building, and by a man whose methods I never particularly admired.

GELLBURG: Yes, that's what I mean. But I had nothing to do with Kershowitz . . .

Breaks off into silence.

CASE: But did I say you did? I'm not clear about what you wanted to say to me, or have I missed some . . . ?

GELLBURG: No—no, just that. What you just said.

CASE, *his mystification peaking:* What's the matter with you?

GELLBURG: I'm sorry. I'd like to forget the whole thing.

CASE: What's happening?

GELLBURG: Nothing. Really.

Case marches out. Gellburg is left open-mouthed, one hand raised as though to bring back his life.

Blackout.

SCENE EIGHT

The cellist plays and is gone.

Sylvia in a wheelchair is listening to Eddie Cantor on the radio, singing "If You Knew Susie Like I Know Susie." She has an amused look, taps a finger to the rhythm. Her bed is nearby, on it a folded newspaper.

Hyman appears. She instantly smiles, turns off the radio and holds a hand out to him. He comes and shakes hands.

SYLVIA, *indicating the radio:* I simply can't stand Eddie Cantor, can you?

HYMAN: Cut it out now, I heard you laughing halfway up the stairs.

SYLVIA: I know, but I can't stand him. This Crosby's the one I like. You ever hear him?

HYMAN: I can't stand these crooners—they're making ten, twenty thousand dollars a week and never spent a day in medical school. *Sylvia laughs.* Anyway, I'm an opera man.

SYLVIA: I never saw an opera. They must be hard to understand, I bet.

HYMAN: Nothing to understand—either she wants to and he doesn't or he wants to and she doesn't. *Sylvia laughs.* Either way one of them gets killed and the other one jumps off a building.

SYLVIA: I'm so glad you could come.

HYMAN, *settling into chair near the bed:* —You ready? I want to ask you a question.

SYLVIA: Phillip had to go to Jersey for a zoning meeting . . .

HYMAN: Just as well—it's a question for you.

SYLVIA: —There's some factory the firm owns there . . .

HYMAN: Come on, don't be nervous.

SYLVIA: . . . My back aches, will you help me onto the bed?

HYMAN: Sure.

She grips him around the shoulders.

There we go.

. . . *and Hyman swings her onto the bed and she lies back. He leaves the bedside.*

What's that perfume?

SYLVIA: Harriet found it in my drawer. I think Jerome bought it for one of my birthdays years ago.

HYMAN: Lovely. Your hair is different.

SYLVIA, *puffs up her hair:* Harriet did it; she's loved playing with my hair since we were kids. Did you hear all those birds this morning?

HYMAN: Amazing, yes; a whole cloud of them shot up like a spray in front of my horse.

SYLVIA, *partially to keep him:* You know, as a child, when we first moved from upstate there were so many birds and rabbits and even foxes here. —Of course that was *real* country up there; my Dad had a wonderful general store, everything from ladies hats to horseshoes. But the winters were just finally too cold for my mother.

HYMAN: In Coney Island we used to kill rabbits with slingshots.

SYLVIA, *wrinkling her nose in disgust:* Why!

HYMAN, *shrugs:* —To see if we could. It was heaven for kids.

SYLVIA: I know! Brooklyn was really beautiful, wasn't it? I think people were happier then. My mother used to stand on our porch and watch us all the way to school, right across open fields for— must have been a mile. And I would tie a clothesline around my three sisters so I wouldn't have to keep chasing after them! —I'm so glad—honestly. *A cozy little laugh.* I feel good every time you come.

HYMAN: Now listen to me; I've learned that your kind of symptoms come from very deep in the mind. I would have to deal with your dreams to get any results, your deepest secret feelings, you understand?

SYLVIA: But when you talk to me I really feel my strength starting to come back . . .

HYMAN: You should already be having therapy to keep up your circulation.

A change in Sylvia's expression, a sudden withdrawal which Hyman notices.

You have a long life ahead of you, you don't want to live it in a wheelchair, do you?

SYLVIA: I could tell you a dream.

HYMAN: I'm not trained to . . .

SYLVIA: I'd like to, can I? —I have the same one every night just as I'm falling asleep.

HYMAN: Well . . . All right, what is it?

SYLVIA: I'm in a street. Everything is sort of gray. And there's a crowd of people. They're packed in all around, and they're looking for me.

HYMAN: Who are they?

SYLVIA: They're Germans.

HYMAN: Sounds like those photographs in the papers.

SYLVIA, *discovering it now:* I think so, yes!

HYMAN: Does something happen?

SYLVIA: Well, I begin to run away. And the whole crowd is chasing after me. They have heavy shoes that pound on the pavement. Then just as I'm escaping around a corner a man catches me and pushes me down . . . *Breaks off.*

HYMAN: Is that the end of it?

SYLVIA: No. He gets on top of me, and begins kissing me . . . *Breaks off.*

HYMAN: Yes?

SYLVIA: . . . And then he starts to cut off my breasts. And he raises himself up, and for a second I see the side of his face.

HYMAN: Who is it?

SYLVIA: . . . I don't know.

HYMAN: But you saw his face.

SYLVIA: I think it's Phillip. *Pause.* But how could Phillip be like . . . he was almost like one of the others?

HYMAN: I don't know. Why do you think?

SYLVIA: Would it be possible . . . because Phillip . . . I mean . . . *A little laugh* . . . he sounds sometimes like he doesn't like Jews? *Correcting.* Of course he doesn't *mean* it, but maybe in my mind it's like he's . . . *Breaks off.*

HYMAN: Like he's what. What's frightening you?

Sylvia is silent, turns away.

   Sylvia?

Hyman tries to turn her face towards him, but she resists. Sylvia is unable to speak.

   Not Phillip, is it?

Sylvia turns to him, the answer is in her eyes. He is amazed. He stands, moves from the bed and halts, trying to weigh this added complication.

   I see.

Returning to the bed, sits, takes her hand.

I see. *Returning to the bed, sits, takes her hand.*

SYLVIA, *she draws Hyman to her and kisses him on the mouth:* I can't help it.

She bursts into tears.

HYMAN: Oh God, Sylvia, I'm so sorry . . .

SYLVIA: Help me. Please!

HYMAN: I'm trying to.

SYLVIA: I know!

She weeps even more deeply. With a desperate cry filled with her pain she embraces him desperately.

HYMAN: Oh Sylvia, Sylvia . . . Here . . .

Hyman gives her his handkerchief. She wipes her face. He smooths back a strand of her hair.

SYLVIA: I feel so foolish.

HYMAN: No-no. You're unhappy, not foolish.

SYLVIA: I feel like I'm losing everything, I'm being torn to pieces. What do you want to know, I'll tell you!

Cries into her hands. He moves, trying to make a decision . . .

I trust you. What did you want to ask me?

HYMAN: —Since this happened to you, have you and Phillip had relations?

SYLVIA, *open surprise:* Relations?

HYMAN: He said you did the other night.

SYLVIA: We had *relations* the other night?

HYMAN: But that . . . well, he said that by morning you'd forgotten. Is that true?

Sylvia is motionless, looking past him with immense uncertainty.

SYLVIA, *alarmed sense of rejection:* Why are you asking me that?

HYMAN: I didn't know what to make of it . . . I guess I still don't.

SYLVIA, *deeply embarrassed:* You mean you believe him?

HYMAN: Well . . . I didn't know what to believe.

SYLVIA: You must think I'm crazy, —to forget a such a thing.

HYMAN: Oh God no! —I didn't mean anything like that . . .

SYLVIA: We haven't had relations for almost twenty years.

The shock pitches him into silence. Now he doesn't know what or who to believe.

HYMAN: Twenty . . . ?

SYLVIA: Just after Jerome was born.

HYMAN: I just . . . I don't know what to say, Sylvia.

SYLVIA: You never heard of it before with people?

HYMAN: Yes, but not when they're as young as you.

SYLVIA: You might be surprised.

HYMAN: What was it, another woman, or what?

SYLVIA: Oh no.

HYMAN: Then what happened?

SYLVIA: I don't know, I never understood it. He just couldn't any-more.

Sylvia tries to read his reaction; Hyman doesn't face her directly.

You believe me, don't you?

HYMAN: Of course I do. But why would he invent a story like that?

SYLVIA, *incredulously:* I can't imagine . . . Could he be trying to
. . . *Breaks off*

HYMAN: What.

SYLVIA: . . . Make you think I've gone crazy?

HYMAN: No, you mustn't believe that. I think maybe . . . you see,
he mentioned my so called reputation with women, and maybe he
was just trying to look . . . I don't know—competitive. How did
this start? Was there some reason?

SYLVIA: I think I made one mistake. He hadn't come near me for like
—I don't remember anymore—a month maybe; and . . . I was
so young . . . a man to me was so much stronger that I couldn't
imagine I could . . . you know, hurt him like that.

HYMAN: Like what?

SYLVIA: Well . . . *Small laugh.* I mentioned it to my father—who
loved Phillip—and he took him aside and tried to suggest a doctor. I should never have mentioned it, it was a terrible mistake,
for a while I thought we'd have to have a divorce . . . it was
months before he could say good morning he was so furious. I
finally got him to go with me to Rabbi Steiner, but he just sat
there like a . . . *Sylvia sighs, shakes her head.*—I don't know, I
guess you just gradually give up and it closes over you like a
grave. But I can't help it, I still pity him; because I know how it
tortures him, it's like a snake eating into his heart . . . I mean
it's not as though he doesn't like me, he does, I know it. —Or do
you think so?

HYMAN: He says you're his whole life. *She is staring, shaking her head, stunned.*

SYLVIA, *with bitter irony:* His whole life! Poor Phillip. —I guess you're right—he was ashamed in front of you, so he made that up.

HYMAN: I've been talking to a friend of mine in the hospital, a psychiatrist. I want your permission to bring him in; I'll call you in the morning.

SYLVIA, *instantly:* Why must you leave? I'm nervous now. Can't you talk to me a few minutes? Come and sit. —Tell me about Germany; you were really there four years?

HYMAN, *sits on the bed:* —The best years of my life.

SYLVIA: And you really made friends with them?

HYMAN: Lots of them. You know, German music and literature is some of the greatest in the world; it's impossible for those people to suddenly change into thugs like this. This will all pass, Sylvia, so you ought to have more confidence, you see? —I mean in general, in life, in people.

SYLVIA, *sucking up reassurance from him:* I have some yeast cake. I'll make fresh coffee . . .

HYMAN: I'd love to stay but Margaret'll be upset with me.

SYLVIA: Oh. Well call her! Ask her to come over too.

HYMAN: No-no . . .

SYLVIA, *a sudden anxiety-burst, colored by her feminine disappointment:* For God's sake, why not!

HYMAN: She thinks something's going on with us.

SYLVIA, *pleased surprise—and worriedly:* Oh!

HYMAN: I'll be in touch tomorrow . . .

SYLVIA: Couldn't you just be here when he comes.

Her anxiety forces him back down on the bed. She takes his hand.

HYMAN: You don't think he'd do something, do you?

SYLVIA: I've never known him so angry. —And I think there's also some trouble with Mr. Case. Phillip can hit, you know. *Shakes her head.* God, everything's so mixed up! *Pause. Sylvia sits there shaking her head, then lifts the newspaper.* But I don't understand— they write that the Germans are starting to pick up Jews right off the street and putting them into . . .

HYMAN, *impatience:* Now Sylvia, I told you . . .

SYLVIA: But you say they were such nice people—how could they change like this!

HYMAN: I don't know! —But . . . here, let me tell you something; I spent a two-month vacation in Paris and the French were much more anti-Semitic. Much more. 1927, November and December. In fact, I would say Germany then was probably better than any other country in Europe.

SYLVIA: But that's what I mean, what *happened* to them?

Slight pause.

HYMAN, *Sylvia stares at him, becoming transformed:* What are you telling me? Just say what you're thinking right now.

SYLVIA, *she has become terrified:* You.

HYMAN: Me! What about me?

SYLVIA: How could you believe I forgot we had relations?

HYMAN: I didn't say I believed it, but I had to ask you since Phillip said it.

SYLVIA: But you believed him a little, didn't you—that I'm crazy . . .

HYMAN, *her persistent intensity unnerving him:* Now stop that! I was only trying to understand what is happening.

SYLVIA, *shouting; his incomprehension dangerous:* But how can those nice people go out and pick Jews off the street in the middle of a big city like that, and nobody stops them . . . ?

HYMAN, *mystified; he takes her hand, and indicates the newspaper:* What has Germany got to do with your condition?

SYLVIA: You could help me if you believed me!

HYMAN, *his spine tingling with her fear; a shout:* I do believe you!

SYLVIA: No! —You're not going to put me away somewhere!

HYMAN, *a horrified shout:* Now you stop being ridiculous!

SYLVIA: But . . . but what . . . what . . . *Gripping her head; his uncertainty terrifying her.* What will become of us!

HYMAN, *unnerved:* Now stop it—you are confusing two things . . . !

SYLVIA: But . . . from now on . . . you mean if a Jew walks out of his house, do they arrest him . . . ?

HYMAN: I'm telling you this won't last.

SYLVIA: But what do they do with them?

HYMAN: I don't know! I'm out of my depth! I can't help you! *He strides to the periphery.*

SYLVIA: But why don't they run out of the country!

The passionate incongruity stops him.

What is the matter with those people! Don't you understand . . . ? *Screaming.* . . . This is an *emergency!* They are beating up little children! What if they kill those children!

Sylvia's outcry continuing, she flings off the blanket and gripping her thighs quickly pulls her legs over the edge of the bed in an hysterical attempt to reach Hyman and the power she feels in him.

Where is Roosevelt! Where is England! You've got to do something before they murder us all!

Sylvia takes a step off the edge of the bed and she collapses on the floor. Hyman catches her, lifts her on to the bed and lightly slaps her cheeks.

HYMAN: Sylvia? Sylvia!

Gellburg enters.

GELLBURG: What happened!

HYMAN: Run cold water on a towel!

GELLBURG: What happened!

HYMAN: Do it, God damn you!

Gellburg rushes out.

Sylvia!—Oh good, that's it, keep looking at me, that's it, keep your eyes open . . .

Gellburg hurries in with a towel and gives it to Hyman who presses it onto her forehead and back of her neck.

There we are, that's better, how do you feel, can you speak? You want to sit up? Come.

He helps her to sit up. She looks around and then at Phillip.

GELLBURG, *to Hyman:* Did *she* call *you?*

HYMAN, *hesitates; and in an angry tone . . . :* Well no, to tell the truth.

GELLBURG: Then what are you doing here?

HYMAN: I stopped by, I was worried about her.

GELLBURG: You were worried about her. Why were you worried about her?

HYMAN, *anger is suddenly sweeping him:* Because she is desperate to be loved.

GELLBURG, *off guard, astonished:* You don't say!

HYMAN: Yes, I do say. *To her.* I want you to try to move your legs. Try it.

Sylvia tries; nothing happens.

I'll be at home if you need me; don't be afraid to call anytime. We'll talk about this more tomorrow. Good night.

SYLVIA, *faintly, afraid:* Good night.

Hyman gives Gellburg a quick, outraged glance. Hyman leaves.

GELLBURG, *reaching for his authority:* That's some attitude he's got, ordering me around like that. I'm going to see about getting somebody else tomorrow. Jersey seems to get further and further away, I'm exhausted.

SYLVIA: I almost started walking.

GELLBURG: What are you talking about?

SYLVIA: For a minute. I don't know what happened, my strength it started to come back.

GELLBURG: I knew it! I told you you could! Try it again, come.

SYLVIA, *she tries to raise her legs:* I can't now.

GELLBURG: Why not! Come, this is wonderful . . . ! *Gellburg reaches for her.*

SYLVIA: Phillip listen . . . I don't want to change, I want Hyman.

GELLBURG, *his purse-mouthed grin:* What's so good about him?— You're still laying there, practically dead to the world.

SYLVIA: He helped me get up, I don't know why. I feel he can get me walking again.

GELLBURG: Why does it have to be him?

SYLVIA: Because I can talk to him! I want *him. An outbreak.* And I don't want to discuss it again!

GELLBURG: Well we'll see.

SYLVIA: We will not see!

GELLBURG: What's this tone of voice?

SYLVIA, *trembling out of control:* It's a Jewish woman's tone of voice!

GELLBURG: A Jewish woman . . . ! What are you talking about, are you crazy?

SYLVIA: Don't you call me crazy, Phillip! I'm talking about it! They are smashing windows and beating children! I am talking about it! *Screams at Gellburg.* I am talking about it, Phillip!

She grips her head in her confusion. He is stock still; horrified, fearful.

GELLBURG: What . . . "beating children?"

SYLVIA: Never mind. Don't sleep with me again.

GELLBURG: How can you say that to me?

SYLVIA: I can't bear it. You give me terrible dreams. I'm sorry, Phillip. Maybe in a while but not now.

GELLBURG, *comes to the bed, goes to his knees clasping his hands together:* Sylvia, you will kill me if we can't be together . . .

SYLVIA: You told him we had relations?

GELLBURG, *beginning to weep:* Don't, Sylvia . . . !

SYLVIA: You little liar! —You want him to think I'm crazy? Is that it? *Now she breaks into weeping.*

GELLBURG: No! It just . . . it came out, I didn't know what I was saying!

SYLVIA: *That I forgot we had relations?! Phillip?*

GELLBURG: Stop that! Don't say anymore.

SYLVIA: I'm going to say anything I want to.

GELLBURG, *weeping:* You will kill me . . . !

They are silent for a moment.

SYLVIA: What I did with my life! Out of ignorance. Out of not wanting to shame you in front of other people. A whole life. Gave it away like a couple of pennies— I took better care of my shoes. *Turns to him.*— You want to talk to me about it now? Take me seriously,

Phillip. What happened? I know it's all you ever thought about, isn't that true? *What happened?* Just so I'll know.

A long pause.

GELLBURG: I'm ashamed to mention it. It's ridiculous.

SYLVIA: What are you talking about?

GELLBURG: It was a mistake. But I was ignorant, I couldn't help myself. —When you said you wanted to go back to the firm.

SYLVIA: What are you talking about? —When?

GELLBURG: When you had Jerome . . . and suddenly you didn't want to keep the house anymore.

SYLVIA: And? —You didn't want me to go back to business, so I didn't.

He doesn't speak; her rage an inch below.

Well what? I didn't, did I?

GELLBURG: You held it against me, having to stay home, you know you did. You've probably forgotten, but not a day passed, not a person could come into this house that you didn't keep saying how wonderful and interesting it used to be for you in business. You never forgave me, Sylvia.

She evades his gaze.

So whenever I . . . when I started to touch you, I felt that.

SYLVIA: You felt what?

GELLBURG: That you didn't want me to be the man here. And then, on top of that when you didn't want any more children . . . everything inside me just dried up. And maybe it was also that to me it was a miracle you ever married me in the first place.

SYLVIA: You mean your face?

He turns slightly.

What have you got against your face? A Jew can have a Jewish face.

Pause.

GELLBURG: I can't help my thoughts, nobody can . . . I admit it was a mistake, I tried a hundred times to talk to you, but I couldn't. I kept waiting for myself to change. Or you. And then we got to where it didn't seem to matter anymore. So I left it that way. And I couldn't change anything anymore.

Pause.

SYLVIA: This is a whole life we're talking about.

GELLBURG: But couldn't we . . . if I taught you to drive and you could go anywhere you liked . . . Or maybe you could find a position you liked . . . ?

Sylvia is staring ahead.

We have to sleep together.

SYLVIA: No.

GELLBURG: How can this be?

Sylvia is motionless.

Sylvia? *Pause.* Do you want to kill me?

Sylvia is staring ahead, Gellburg is watching and awaiting her reply. He shouts.

Is that it! Speak to me!

Sylvia's face is blank, unreadable, she turns to Gellburg saying nothing.

Blackout.

SCENE NINE

Case enters. His manner is formal and cold. He stands before Gellburg who has gotten to his feet.

CASE: Good morning, Gellburg.

GELLBURG: Good morning, Mr. Case.

CASE: I understand you wish to see me.

GELLBURG: There was just something I felt I should say.

CASE: Certainly. *Case goes to a chair and sits.* Yes?

GELLBURG: It's just that I would never in this world do anything against you or Brooklyn Guarantee. I don't have to tell you, it's the only place I've ever worked in my life. My whole life is here. I'm more proud of this company than almost anything except my own son. What I'm trying to say is that this whole business with Wanamaker's was only because I didn't want to leave a stone unturned. Two or three years from now I didn't want you waking up one morning and Wanamaker's is gone and there you are paying New York taxes on a building in the middle of a dying neighborhood.

Case lets Gellburg hang there. Gellburg begins to get flustered.

Frankly, I don't even remember what this whole thing was about. I feel I've lost some of your confidence, and it's . . . well, it's unfair, I feel.

CASE: I understand.

GELLBURG, *he waits, but that's it:* But . . . but don't you believe me?

CASE: I think I do.

GELLBURG: But . . . you seem to be . . . you don't seem . . .

CASE: The fact remains that I've lost the building.

GELLBURG: But are you . . . I mean you're not still thinking that I had something going on with Allan Kershowitz, are you?

CASE: Put it this way— I hope as time goes on that my old confidence will return. That's about as far as I can go, and I don't think you can blame me, can you. *Case stands.*

GELLBURG, *despite himself his voice rises:* But how can I work if you're this way? You have to trust a man, don't you?

CASE, *begins to indicate he must leave:* I'll have to ask you to . . .

GELLBURG: I don't deserve this! This is not fair, Mr. Case! I had nothing to do with Allan Kershowitz! I hardly know the man! And the little I do know I don't even like him, I'd certainly never get into a deal with him, for God's sake! This is . . . this whole thing is . . . *Exploding.* I don't understand it, what is happening, what the hell is happening, what have I got to do with Allan Kershowitz, just because he's also a Jew?

CASE, *incredulously and angering:* What? What on earth are you talking about!

GELLBURG: Excuse me. I didn't mean that.

CASE: I don't understand . . . how could you say a thing like that!

GELLBURG: Please. I don't feel well, excuse me . . .

CASE, *his resentment mounting:* But how could you say such a thing!
It's an outrage, Gellburg!

*Gellburg takes a step to leave and goes to his knees, his head hanging
between his arms as he tries to breathe. Case hurries to him.*

CASE: What is it? Gellburg? *Case springs up and goes to the periphery.* Call an ambulance! Hurry, for God's sake! *He rushes out,
shouting.* Quick, get a doctor! It's Gellburg! Gellburg has collapsed!

*Gellburg remains on his hands and knees trying to keep from falling
over, gasping.*

Blackout.

SCENE TEN

Cellist plays, the music falls away.

Gellburg's bedroom. He is in bed. Hyman is listening to Gellburg's heart. Now he puts his stethoscope back into his bag, and sits on a chair beside the bed.

HYMAN: I can only tell you again, Phillip—you belong in the hospital, you simply must go back.

GELLBURG: Please don't argue about it anymore! I couldn't stand it there, it smells like a zoo; and to lay in a bed where some stranger died . . . I hate it. If I'm going out I'll go from here. And I don't want to leave Sylvia.

HYMAN: I'm trying to help you. *Chuckles.* And I'm going to go on trying if it kills both of us.

GELLBURG: I appreciate that. I mean it. You're a good man.

HYMAN: You're lucky I know that. The nurse should be here around six.

GELLBURG: I'm wondering if I need her—I think the pain is practically gone.

HYMAN: I want her here overnight. But I'd still like you back in the hospital.

GELLBURG: I . . . I want to tell you something; when I collapsed
. . . it was like an explosion went off in my head, like a tremendous white light. It sounds funny but I felt a . . . happiness
. . . that funny? Like I suddenly had something to tell her that
would change everything, and we would go back to how it was
when we started out together. I couldn't wait to tell it to her . . .
and now I can't remember what it was. *Anguished, a rushed quality; suddenly near tears.* God, I always thought there'd be time to
get to the bottom of myself!

HYMAN: You might have years, nobody can predict.

GELLBURG: It's unbelievable—the first time since I was twenty I
don't have a job. I just can't believe it.

HYMAN: You sure? Maybe you can clear it up with your boss when
you go back.

GELLBURG: How can I go back? He made a fool of me. It's infuriating.
I tell you—I never wanted to see it this way but he goes sailing
around on the ocean and meanwhile I'm foreclosing Brooklyn for
them. That's what it boils down to. You got some lousy rotten job
to do, get Gellburg, send in the Yid. Close down a business, throw
somebody out of his home . . . And now to accuse me . . .

HYMAN: But is all this news to you? That's the system, isn't it?

GELLBURG: But to accuse me of double-crossing the *company!* That is
absolutely unfair . . . it was like a hammer between the eyes. I
mean to me Brooklyn Guarantee—for God's sake, Brooklyn Guarantee was like . . . like . . .

HYMAN: You're getting too excited, Phillip . . . come on now.
Changing the subject.—I understand your son is coming back
from the Philippines.

GELLBURG, *he catches his breath for a moment:* . . . She show you
his telegram? He's trying to make it here by Monday. *Scared eyes
and a grin.* Or will I last till Monday?

HYMAN: You've got to start thinking about more positive things—seriously, your system needs a rest.

GELLBURG: Who's that talking?

HYMAN, *indicating upstage:* I asked Margaret to sit with your wife for a while, they're in your son's bedroom.

GELLBURG: Do you always take so much trouble?

HYMAN: I like Sylvia.

GELLBURG, *his little grin:* I know . . . I didn't think it was for my sake.

HYMAN: You're not so bad. I have to get back to my office now.

GELLBURG: Please if you have a few minutes, I'd appreciate it. *Almost holding his breath.* Tell me— The thing she's so afraid of . . . is me isn't it?

HYMAN: Well . . . among other things.

GELLBURG, *shock:* It's me?

HYMAN: I think so . . . partly.

GELLBURG, *pressing his fingers against his eyes to regain control:* How could she be frightened of me! I worship her! *Quickly controlling.* How could everything turn out to be the opposite—I made my son in this bed and now I'm dying in it . . . *Breaks off, downing a cry.* My thoughts keep flying around—everything from years ago keeps coming back like it was last week. Like the day we bought this bed. Abraham & Strauss. It was so sunny and beautiful. I took the whole day off. God, it's almost twenty-five years ago! . . . Then we had a soda at Schrafft's—of course they don't hire Jews but the chocolate ice cream is the best. Then we went over to Orchard Street for bargains. Bought our first pots and sheets, blankets, pillowcases. The street was full of pushcarts and men with long beards like a hundred years ago. It's funny, I felt so at home and happy there that day, a street full of Jews, one Moses after another. But they all turned to watch her go by, those fakers. She was a knockout; sometimes walking down the street I couldn't believe I was married to her. Listen . . . *Breaks off; with some diffidence.* You're an educated man, I only went to high school—I wish we could talk about the Jews.

HYMAN: I never studied the history, if that's what you . . .

GELLBURG: . . . I don't know where I am . . .

HYMAN: You mean as a Jew?

GELLBURG: Do you think about it much? I never . . . for instance, a Jew in love with horses is something I never heard of.

HYMAN: My grandfather in Odessa was a horse dealer.

GELLBURG: You don't say! I wouldn't know you were Jewish except for your name.

HYMAN: I have cousins up near Syracuse who are still in the business —they break horses. You know there are Chinese Jews.

GELLBURG: I heard of that! And they look Chinese?

HYMAN: They are Chinese. They'd probably say you don't look Jewish.

GELLBURG: Ha! That's funny. *His laugh disappears; he stares.* Why is it so hard to be a Jew?

HYMAN: It's hard to be anything.

GELLBURG: No, it's different for them. Being a Jew is a full-time job. Except you don't think about it much, do you. —Like when you're on your horse, or . . .

HYMAN: It's not an obsession for me . . .

GELLBURG: But how'd you come you marry a shiksa?

HYMAN: We were thrown together when I was interning, and we got very close, and . . . well, she was a good partner, she helped me, and still does. And I loved her.

GELLBURG:—A Jewish woman couldn't help you?

HYMAN: Sure. But it just didn't happen

GELLBURG: It wasn't so you wouldn't seem Jewish?

HYMAN, *coldly:* I never pretended I wasn't Jewish.

GELLBURG, *almost shaking with some fear:* Look, don't be mad, I'm only trying to figure out . . .

HYMAN, *sensing the underlying hostility:* What are you driving at, I don't understand this whole conversation.

GELLBURG: Hyman, help me! I've never been so afraid in my life.

HYMAN: If you're alive you're afraid; we're born afraid—a newborn baby is not a picture of confidence; but how you deal with fear, that's what counts. I don't think you dealt with it very well.

GELLBURG: Why? How did I deal with it?

HYMAN: I think you tried to disappear into the Goyim.

GELLBURG: . . . You believe in God?

HYMAN: I'm a Socialist. I think we're at the end of religion.

GELLBURG: You mean everybody working for the government.

HYMAN: It's the only future that makes any rational sense.

GELLBURG: God forbid. But how can there be Jews if there's no God?

HYMAN: Oh, they'll find something to worship. The Christians will too—maybe different brands of ketchup.

GELLBURG, *laughs:* Boy, the things you come out with sometimes . . . !

HYMAN: —Someday we're all going to look like a lot of monkeys running around trying to figure out a coconut.

GELLBURG: Hyman . . . I think the pain is coming again.

HYMAN: Be quiet. *Takes out his stethoscope, places on Gellburg's chest.*

GELLBURG: She believes in you, Hyman . . .

HYMAN: Sssh.

GELLBURG: . . . I want you to tell her—tell her I'm going to change. She has no right to be so frightened. Of me or anything else. They will never destroy us. When the last Jew dies the light of the world will go out. She has to understand that—those Germans are shooting at the sun!

HYMAN: Be quiet.

GELLBURG, *overriding his embarrassment—quietly from the center of his soul:* I want my wife back. I want her back before something happens. I feel like there's nothing inside me, I feel empty. I want her back.

HYMAN: Phillip, what can I do about that?

GELLBURG: Never mind . . . since you started coming around . . . in those boots . . . like some kind of horseback rider . . . ?

HYMAN: What the hell are you talking about!

GELLBURG: Since you came around she looks down at me like a miserable piece of shit!

HYMAN: Phillip . . .

GELLBURG: Don't "Phillip" me, just stop it!

HYMAN: Don't scream at me Phillip, you know how to get your wife back! . . . don't tell me there's a mystery to that!

GELLBURG: She actually told you that I. . . .

HYMAN: It came out while we were talking. It was bound to sooner or later, wasn't it?

GELLBURG, *gritting his teeth:* I worshipped her.

HYMAN: Phillip, I've got to send you back to the hospital.

GELLBURG: I never told this to anyone . . . but years ago when I used to make love to her, I would almost feel like a small baby on top of her, like she was giving me birth. That's some idea? In bed next to me she was like a . . . a marble god. I worshipped her, Hyman, from the day I laid eyes on her.

HYMAN: I'm sorry for you Phillip.

GELLBURG: How can she be so afraid of me? Tell me the truth.

HYMAN: I don't know; maybe, for one thing . . . these remarks you're always making about Jews.

GELLBURG: What remarks?

HYMAN: Like not wanting to be mistaken for Goldberg.

GELLBURG: So I'm a Nazi? Is Gellburg Goldberg? It's not is it?

HYMAN: No, but continually making the point is kind of . . .

GELLBURG: Kind of what? What is kind of? Why don't you say the truth?

HYMAN: All right you want the truth? Do you? Look in the mirror sometime!

GELLBURG: . . . In the mirror?

HYMAN: You hate yourself, that's what's scaring her to death. That's my opinion. How's it possible I don't know, but I think you helped paralyze her with this "Jew, Jew, Jew" coming out of your mouth and the same time she reads it in the paper and it's coming out of the radio day and night? You wanted to know what I think . . . that's exactly what I think.

GELLBURG: But there are some days I feel like going and sitting in the Schul with the old men and pulling the *tallis* over my head and be a full-time Jew the rest of my life. With the sidelocks and the black hat, and settle it once and for all. And other times . . . yes, I could almost kill them. They infuriate me. I am ashamed of them and that I look like them. *Gasping again.* —Why must we be different? Why is it? What is it for?

HYMAN: And supposing it turns out that we're *not* different, who are you going to blame then?

GELLBURG: What are you talking about?

HYMAN: I'm talking about all this grinding and screaming that's going on inside you—you're wearing yourself out for nothing, Phillip, absolutely nothing! —I'll tell you a secret—I have all kinds coming into my office, and there's not one of them who one way or another is not persecuted. Yes. *Everybody's* persecuted. The poor by the rich, the rich by the poor, the black by the white, the white by the black, the men by the women, the women by the men, the Catholics by the Protestants, the Protestants by the Catholics— and of course all of them by the Jews. Everybody's persecuted— sometimes I wonder, maybe that's what holds this country together! And what's really amazing is that you can't find anybody who's persecuting anybody else.

GELLBURG: So you mean there's no Hitler?

HYMAN: Hitler? Hitler is the perfect example of the persecuted man! I've heard him—he kvetches like an elephant was standing on his pecker! They've turned that whole beautiful country into one gigantic kvetch!

GELLBURG: So what's the solution?

HYMAN: I don't see any. Except the mirror. But nobody's going to look at himself and ask what am *I* doing—you might as well tell him to take a seat in the hottest part of hell. *Takes his bag.* Forgive her, Phillip, is all I really know to tell you. *Grins.* But that's the easy part—I speak from experience.

GELLBURG: What's the hard part?

HYMAN: To forgive yourself, I guess. And the Jews. And while you're at it, you can throw in the Goyim. Best thing for the heart you know.

Sylvia enters, Margaret pushing the chair. To Sylvia . . .

I want him in the hospital tonight for observation. I'm going down to arrange for an ambulance. To Gellburg. And don't argue.

Hyman exits.

MARGARET: I'll leave you now, Sylvia.

SYLVIA: Thanks for sitting with me.

GELLBURG, *a little wave of the hand:* Thank you Mrs. Hyman!

MARGARET: I think your color's coming back a little.

GELLBURG: Well, I've been running around the block.

MARGARET, *a burst of laughter and shaking her finger at him:* I always knew there was a sense of humor somewhere inside that black suit!

GELLBURG: Yes, well . . . I finally got the joke. —And besides, with that laugh, who can resist?

MARGARET, *laughs, and to Sylvia:* I'll try to look in tomorrow. *To both.* Goodbye!

Margaret exits. A silence between them grows self-conscious.

GELLBURG: You all right in that room?

SYLVIA: It's better this way, we'll both get more rest. You all right?

GELLBURG: I want to apologize.

SYLVIA: I'm not blaming you, Phillip. The years I wasted. I know I threw it away myself. I think I always knew why I was doing it but I couldn't stop it.

GELLBURG: If only you could believe I never meant you harm, it would . . .

SYLVIA: I believe you. But I have to tell you something. When I said not to sleep with me . . .

GELLBURG: I know . . .

SYLVIA, *nervously sharp:* You don't know! —I'm trying to tell you something! *Containing herself.* Maybe it was talking to the doctor that reminded me how I used to be; remember my parents' house, how full of love it always was? Nobody was ever afraid of anything. But with us, Phillip, everything somehow got . . . dangerous. Whatever I wanted to do, whatever I wanted to say, I had to tiptoe around you. And it wasn't me. *With disgust indicates her legs.* And this isn't! I am not this thing that can't even walk. *Pounding on her thighs.* I am not this thing!

GELLBURG: Sshh! I understand. I wasn't telling you the truth. I always tried to seem otherwise, but I've been more afraid than I looked.

SYLVIA: Afraid of what?

GELLBURG: Everything. Of Germany. Mr. Case. Of what could happen to us here. I think I was more afraid than you are, a hundred times more! And in the meantime there are Chinese Jews, for God's sake.

SYLVIA: What do you mean?

GELLBURG: They're *Chinese!*—and here I spend a lifetime looking in the mirror at my face! —Why we're different I will never understand but to live so afraid, I don't want that anymore. I tell you, if I live I have to try to change myself. —Sylvia, my darling Sylvia, I'm asking you not to blame me anymore. Because that's the knife in my heart. Can't you try to stand up? I feel I did this to you!

Gellburg's breathing begins to labor.

SYLVIA, *pressing down on the chair arms:* I would do it but I can't!

GELLBURG: Try it! God almighty, Sylvia forgive me!

A paroxysm forces Gellburg up to a nearly sitting position.

SYLVIA, *struggling to rise:* Wait! Phillip, look, I'm walking!

Sylvia's feet on the floor, she is struggling to break free of the chair's support.

There's nothing to blame! I'm all right! Look, I'm all right! Look at me!

Phillip falls back dead. Sylvia is desperately struggling to stand and get over to him. And as she struggles to balance herself on her legs . . .

Wait, wait . . . !

LIGHTS FADE.

THE END.